Dorothea Lange

Hopi Indian, New Mexico, c. 1923

Dorothea Lange

Photographs of a Lifetime

with an Essay
by ROBERT COLES

Afterword by Therese Heyman

AN APERTURE MONOGRAPH

Library of Congress Card Catalogue No. 82-70769
ISBN 0-89381-100-9. *Published by Aperture, Inc.*
Distributed in the United States by Viking Penguin, Inc.;
in the United Kingdom, Commonwealth, and other
world markets by Phaidon Press Limited, Oxford; in Canada by
Van Nostrand Reinhold, Ltd., Ontario; and in Italy by Idea Books, Milan.

Staff for Dorothea Lange: Photographs of a Lifetime:
Editor-Publisher, Michael E. Hoffman; Associate Editor, Carole Kismaric;
Special Project Editor, R. H. Cravens; Production Manager, Charles Gershwin;
Designer, Wendy Byrne; Editorial Assistant, Scott Rucker.

Dorothea Lange: Photographs of Lifetime *is supported by grants from*
the Florence M. Burden Foundation and the Paul Strand Foundation.

Aperture, Inc., a public foundation, publishes a periodical,
portfolios, and books to communicate with serious
photographers and creative people everywhere. A complete
catalogue will be mailed upon request.
Address: Aperture, Inc., Millerton, New York 12546
Aperture, Inc., 20 East 23 Street, New York, New York 10010

Second Printing
Composition by David E. Seham Associates, Inc., Metuchen,
New Jersey. Duotone negatives by Richard M. A. Benson.
Printing by Amilcare Pizzi S.p.A. Printed and bound in Italy.

Contents

You put your camera around your neck in the morning
along with putting on your shoes, and there it is,
an appendage of the body that shares your life with you.
The camera is an instrument that teaches people
how to see without a camera.

You force *yourself to watch and wait. You accept all the*
discomfort and the disharmony. Being out of your depth
is a very uncomfortable thing. . . . You force yourself
onto strange streets, among strangers. It may be very hot.
It may be painfully cold. It may be sandy and windy
and you say, "What am I doing here?
What drives me to do this hard thing?"

Dorothea Lange

Dorothea Lange is one of those rare but recurrent figures in a particular American tradition—the artist drawn to the lives of people otherwise unknown, to places seldom visited, to experiences many would prefer left neglected. Such artists have characteristics uniquely their own, not the least of which is a kind of hobo spirit, a companionable feeling for the down and out. Such artists produce texts or pictures that pulse with moral passion, awakening our own connection to the individuals who are their subjects. Such artists go exactly to the moment, exactly to the situation; they create images or works which acquire a measure of universality. The transcendent power of that work, of course, has to do with the observer's artistic gifts.

Lange was an exceptional photographer before—and often a brilliant one after—the great Depression. Those chaotic years, the vastness of the event, called forth something more in her. Today her images retain their emotional vitality, their faithfulness to the experience, long after the subjects, the circumstance, and the photographer herself have passed from the scene. There are few who possess the intuitive sense necessary for accurate social observation—the identification of the remark, the image, the situation that tells the greater story. There are very few indeed who combine with this capacity the personal vision and developed gifts of the artist. Among Lange's colleagues on the now legendary photography staff of the Farm Security Administration (FSA), there were such artists: Walker Evans and Russell Lee. That fearsome decade of the thirties also kindled the genius waiting in writers such as John Steinbeck, John Dos Passos, and Clifford Odets. They belong to a lineage that stretches back to Mathew Brady and Walt Whitman and forward to Robert Frank and Jack Kerouac, chroniclers of American manners and mores in the fifties. They are more precious than we might imagine, these artist-observers, in the unfolding experience of our society.

William Carlos Williams was another such artist-observer—one I was lucky enough to be able to know. When not squeezing out of his exhaustion the hours to write poems or novels or plays or essays, Dr. Williams walked the streets of Paterson, New Jersey, as a general practitioner. That term is now discarded by physicians for another: "family medicine." He saw families all right, dozens each week. He climbed the stairs of tenement buildings, knocked on old, battered doors, and shouted gruffly the name that always earned him entry: "Doc Williams." He left behind a trail of prescriptions and free samples he'd received from drug companies. Not least, he left down-home advice—he was a sophisticated intellectual who had a knack of putting complicated medical or social issues into terse, catchy phrases.

I had the opportunity to follow him many times on those street rounds, to watch a doctor glide from the "brawl of Paterson," as he described his medical turf, to artistic work. Once he wrote to me:

Doctors need to look more—not try so hard to zero in, make a diagnosis. Sit back, stretch, catch something in the room with your eyes, and don't let go so fast! Don't glance; stare and remember! Well, I'm no teacher, except when I write poems, and then I try to be as indirect as possible. But there's a big world for each of us to greet, and anyone who writes or paints is trying to bring that world closer to other people. It's like saying: hear, see—and pay attention, please. Over and over again. But you try to collar people gently. *You insinuate your vision—and hope it helps a few others to take notice of things. Oh yes,* things. *Like I said in* Paterson, *"say it, no ideas but in things."*

Within that great poem, the doctor-poet put it this way: "Outside/outside myself/there is a world,/he rumbled subject to my incursions/—a world (to me) at rest/which I approach/concretely—" That world, Williams once said, he called upon "like a man regaining his appetite, anxious to eat, but wanting to savor everything, too."

The photographer whose work would resonate so deeply with an appetite for a world "outside myself" was born, coincidentally, within Dr. Williams's clinical range—Hoboken, New Jersey, a city he knew well as a house-visiting physician. At the time of Dorothea Lange's birth, in 1895, Hoboken was, as Williams later described it, a city of "immigrants, from everywhere under the European sun." She was born of such stock, of second-generation German immigrant parents, the first child of Henry and Joan (shortened from Joanna) Nutzhorn, who gave birth to a son, Henry Martin, six years later. Her father was a lawyer, her mother a gentle, beautiful woman who sang in amateur recitals. There was a tradition in the family of the journeyman-artist; three maternal uncles, trained as lithographers in Germany, established a successful business in this country.

Two tragedies tested and shaped the girl. When she was seven she was stricken with polio. The right leg, from the knee down, was impaired. She was called "Limpy" by other children, and for the remainder of her life she would be lame. The handicap haunted her: she accepted but hated it to the end of her life, and at sixty-five she described its significance: "No one who hasn't lived the life of a semi-cripple knows how much that means. I think it was perhaps the most important thing that happened to me. [It] formed me, guided me, instructed me, helped me, and humiliated me. All those things at once. I've never gotten over it and I am aware of the force and power of it."

Many children have been only too willing to find in polio or similar crippling diseases a reason for resignation, if not a withdrawal from the challenges of life. For others, as Dr. Williams described in stories about his patients, there is a redemptive vitality that overwhelms various pains and injuries. In Dorothea, from childhood and throughout life, one gathers, there was a constant effort to make a statement to herself and to others: an impaired gait emphatically does not mean a lagging, curbed life.

When Dorothea was twelve another crisis came upon her: the departure of her father, who walked out, never to return. She never understood why, and could never talk about what happened. There was in her independent nature a habit of closing doors upon past events, of denying the influence of certain experiences and individuals. After the divorce, both daughter and mother adopted Joan's maiden name, Lange. Dorothea kept the secrets of her childhood so well that it was not until after her death that her own husband and children learned that her birthname was Nutzhorn.

Dorothea's mother was left with no money and two small children. She took a job in New York City, as a librarian in a branch of the New York Public Library on the Lower East Side, and enrolled her daughter in nearby Public School 62.

Dorothea and her mother now took the ferry from Hoboken to Manhattan early in the morning, five days a week, into a neighborhood packed with poor people, newly arrived in America. At the time Jacob Riis (*How the Other Half Lives*) and Lewis Hine were both evoking in photographs the vitality, resourcefulness, the desperate circumstances, of lower Manhattan's immigrant life. Suddenly Dorothea was exposed to the likes of Hester Street, the most densely inhabited few blocks in America, crowded with scenes and endless visual excitement. In school, she later recalled, "I was the only Gentile among 3,000 Jews."

If that was an exaggeration, it was an affectionate one. She admired her classmates' ambition, their eagerness to learn. For herself, she was less interested in books than the immediacy of the city's ethnic and cultural life. She became a truant and spent hours roaming through galleries and museums. Lange later remembered as one of the great experiences of her life several successive evenings in the audience when Isadora Duncan danced her legendary performances at the Metropolitan Opera House. But, most of all, she absorbed the sights and sounds and smells of lower-class life in turn-of-the-century New York. By herself, each evening, she walked back along Christopher Street to the ferry, wearing what she called her "cloak of invisibility," acquiring by instinct the craft of being the observer unobserved. Later, she attended irregularly a midtown high school for girls run by "starchy New Englanders." She managed to pass courses and graduate despite what amounted to an aversion for the classroom, for any formal learning situation.

Before she was fully grown, Lange had established the distinctive elements of her later working style: a willingness to inquire relentlessly, to move with ease from neighborhood to neighborhood; an interest in the ability of extremely hard-pressed families nevertheless to make do; the stubborn capacity to negotiate through terrible stresses, if not outright disasters; a defiantly rebellious insistence that her own aesthetic and moral interests be affirmed, no matter the prevailing orthodoxies of others, including parents and school officials; and, particularly, a continual attentiveness—an eye that looked hard and remembered.

Another pattern was being set, too, and it was less appealing. After the breakup of her marriage, Joan had set up housekeeping with her mother. Grandmother Sophie was tyrannical, quarrelsome, often erratic—a fine dressmaker and, apparently, a hard drinker. The curious affinity that so often occurs between alternating generations seems to have happened with Dorothea and Sophie. In later life, Lange, too, was a figure of fearsome authority to her children and stepchildren, often lashing out at them over trivial matters and upon occasion—to her dismay—hearing from her own mouth exactly the same harsh, even unjust words she had once suffered from Sophie. Lange was distressed by her intransigence toward her children, but often unsuccessful in controlling it.

When Dorothea reached her late teens, Joan took on a new job as a court investigator assigned to probation cases. A much older Lange recalled,

I remember my mother going out on streetcars and making night interviews, alone, in all kinds of wretched old Polish tenements in the winter, standing on the windy, snowy street corners at night until late because sometimes she would have to wait until the drunken father came home. I used to like to go with her, to see her walk up the stairs, and knock at a door where "nobody" would be in. She'd listen and she'd know if they were in and not answering. I found myself later sometimes having to knock at a door when I was working and I used to remind myself of my own mother many a time.

That kind of experience, for the artist-observer, is crucially important, utterly instructive. Dr. Williams once cautioned a Harvard undergraduate anxious to launch a career in writing: "I would get away from all those ivy plants. I would run for dear life. I would hurry and find some low-down, hungry, loud-mouthed people, living high in some tenement, plenty of stairs to climb. Let them give you a lecture. Take notes. Keep your eyes open, and close them when you get back to the typewriter, so that you'll be able to retain every detail for yourself."

Dorothea enrolled in the New York Training School for Teachers on 119th Street. Her attendance was a concession to conformity, to her mother's and grandmother's desire for respectability. She was already certain that her life would be spent with a camera. "My mind made itself up," she later recalled, and could add no other explanation for the decision than: "It just came to me that photography would be a good thing for me to do." She was not yet twenty, and she had never owned a camera.

Lange might shun the classroom, but when she wanted to learn she was tenacious, aggressive, and persuasive. She talked her way into a series of apprenticeships, perhaps the most important with Arnold Genthe, who moved to New

York from San Francisco in 1911 and set up a successful portrait studio. In California, Genthe had made portraits of artists, writers, and people of wealth, but he had also documented Chinatown. And when the earthquake of 1906 wrought unparalleled destruction on the Bay Area, Genthe moved amid the rubble. Using a hand-held camera, then a relatively new instrument, he created a landmark of American documentary photography.

Among her other teachers were a succession of "loveable old hacks," including one down-at-the-heels itinerant who knocked on the family's door in 1915, showing his wares and offering to take the family's pictures. With his help, she converted a chicken coop into her first darkroom. Only once as a young woman did she take any formal, academic training in photography. In 1917 she attended a course conducted by Clarence White at Columbia University. A private, somewhat elusive man and a gifted teacher (his students included Doris Ulmann and Laura Gilpin), he influenced Lange at a distance. "He knew," she later recalled, "absolutely when something was beautiful." She could not be bothered with the details of White's assignments—but she absorbed a sense of the purity of his artistry.

Her various apprenticeships completed to her satisfaction, Dorothea prepared for the most defiant act of independence of her life to date. She announced to her mother and grandmother that she intended to travel around the world, paying her way as a photographer. The family objected, but Dorothea could not be stopped. In 1918, accompanied by her childhood friend Florence Ahlstrom—a companion in her truancies from school—she set out for San Francisco. Their first day in the city, the two young women had their savings pilfered from their purses, one of the few times Dorothea was ever careless about money.

Almost immediately, she got a job at a photofinishing company where she took orders for picture enlargements and custom-made frames, and occasionally framed the photographs herself. She began to take her own pictures. One of the first people she met, as a customer who walked through the door, was Roi Partridge, the husband of the photographer Imogen Cunningham. They started a friendship that lasted a lifetime, and through the couple she entered into the social life of San Francisco's bohemian set—writers, painters, photographers, and hangers-on. She received a generous offer that allowed her to achieve her goal of setting up a portrait studio and soon attracted prominent and wealthy sitters to her business on Sutter Street. The clientele was largely drawn from families of the wealthy Jew-

Mrs. Kahn, San Francisco, 1931

Katten Portrait, San Francisco, 1934

ish merchant princes. Years later she would complain of an unfairness: the fame and notoriety of San Francisco's elite had attached to a few mining families, while the Jewish merchants and businessmen truly had created the city's great cultural, artistic, and philanthropic traditions.

It was at Sutter Street, where artists and friends gathered in the evening, that Roi Partridge introduced her to Maynard Dixon. Lange and Dixon were married in the spring of 1920. She was in her mid-twenties, he in his mid-forties. They were a striking couple. She was never a beautiful, perhaps not even a pretty, woman, but her pale, freckled, fine-boned face radiated character and animation. She wore slacks while working, and long, floor-length dresses in the evening, usually with bold, distinctive Indian jewelry. Dixon was a tall, rangy California-born painter and illustrator, respected for his wit, intelligence, and fierce independence. He devoted his artistic energy to the West—its physical contours, its wildlife, its diverse inhabitants. He was an avid traveler, a man who loved to observe others, get to know them, render them on paper and canvas. Dixon's bohemianism had a distinctively Western coloration. He knew Arizona and New Mexico well, and he befriended as well as painted his Hopi and Navajo subjects.

Throughout the early twenties, Dixon and Lange prospered, enjoyed life. His paintings sold well; she was rapidly becoming the best-known portraitist in San Francisco. She had no reputation beyond the city, and she did not consider herself an artist, but she took pride in honest, often charming studies of her clients. The one unhappiness in the family was her inability to respond to the emotional needs of Dixon's daughter by a first marriage. Dorothea applied a certain ferocity to housekeeping: the slightest deviation from her standards, with respect to the keeping of strict schedules or the shaving of a carrot, enraged her. She didn't understand why, but soon her stepchild was living more in the homes of others, a foster child; and it was a pattern that would be repeated.

Ethel Benedict, 1916

Dorothea's first efforts at photographing outside the studio took place in 1922, when she accompanied her husband on a journey through Arizona's high country—small, arid, sparsely inhabited ranch towns, and, of course, the reservations. She took note then of the wretched plight of Indian children—the inadequate, crowded boarding schools they attended, the grim prospects they faced: poverty, joblessness, and, perhaps worst of all, a sense of futility. Theirs was the chronic reservation existence of proud people reduced to ceaseless intimacy with humiliation and defeat. At one stop she took the full-front portrait of a Hopi Indian that became the first powerful image in the Lange opus.

She used her camera on that trip and subsequent ones with no apparent sense of calling, but she was learning. She gradually acquired the knack of moving day after day; of talking with strangers; of absorbing a constantly shifting parade of sights—deserts, canyons, parched rivers, tiny settlements. She discovered a different America in settings that must have jarred eyes accustomed to the narrow, crowded Lower East Side streets, the hills and urbanity of San Francisco.

The Dixon's first son, Daniel, was born in 1925, and a second, John, in 1928. With the children's arrival, strains emerged in the Dixon marriage. Dorothea found it difficult to accommodate herself to the life of an artist's wife and the mother of small boys. She continued working with her affluent clientele, and placed the boys with friends when she and Dixon went on field trips. When she could not travel, his absences stretched into months. Dixon made little effort to disguise his affairs with other women and, perhaps in retaliation, she, too, took lovers.

As the twenties advanced, a worsening national economic situation affected them both; they had less money for photographs, murals, and paintings. Lange often found her husband unnerving, a peculiar mix of snob and populist. He had a good deal of contempt for the bourgeoisie—a traditional artist's pose—and he occasionally ridiculed and played practical jokes on her clients, who increasingly provided the main source of their income. In contrast, Dixon responded warmly to the West's working people and its "minorities." Ranchers, cowboys, and Indians, the proud Hispano-Americans of Taos and Truchas and Madrid and Santa Fe in New Mexico—these were the men and women he judged worthy of his time and interest, his affection and his artist's preoccupation. He was deeply affected by the spectacle of a growing national tragedy: millions of moneyless men, women, and children without adequate shelter or food were drifting, dazed, and frightened, while an ever shrinking minority of the wealthy seemed unwilling to recognize the nature and extent of the scandal.

In 1930 and 1931, in part as a desperate bid to save the marriage, Dixon and Lange spent a lot of time in northern New Mexico. Living for months in Taos, they watched the first of the jobless, homeless families moving through the town. An old Pueblo woman, a child when Lange and Dixon lived there, once vividly described the scene for me:

I was a young woman, then. I had my eyes wide open. I walked into the town, and there they were, people begging, people asking other people for food, for work. And they all had white skin! They weren't from a reservation! I remember asking my mother and my father what was wrong. I remember the smiles on their faces! I remember my mother touching me, both hands on my shoulders, and saying that I should look carefully at the Anglos, the Anglos in the cars that broke down, and the Anglos standing in line, trying to get a job, or some free food. So, I went and looked. They weren't like us! I mean, they were Anglos, of course! But they weren't like us—because they couldn't stay still, and they shouted all the time at each other, and their children were making more noise than I ever heard from people. . . .

No Place to Go, 1935
(painting by Maynard Dixon)

Law and Disorder, 1934
(painting by Maynard Dixon)

Maynard Dixon, 1926

After awhile, I turned away and started home. That was when an Anglo girl–she must have been my age, ten or twelve—came up to me and asked me if my mother and father had some money, and enough food. I said no. If I'd said yes, she would have gone and told her parents, and the other Anglos, and they would have followed me all the way home, I was sure! That was the first and only time I was glad that people were going hungry then, and there wasn't enough cash to buy very much. I guess I was glad (I have to admit it!) because I'd seen Anglos, finally, begging!

Paul Strand was living in Taos at the time. Lange wondered at the concentration of the man who drove by their adobe each day without looking to right or left. She was intimidated, too shy to introduce herself. She had deeply troubled moments about the direction of her own photography. Two years before, she had returned from a field trip almost in despair about the poor quality of her pictures. Perhaps she was experiencing what the French call a "moment of illumination," a vision summoning her to a different kind of work. Here she is, describing that moment to her son Daniel in retrospect:

I was given a big boost by a turbulence of nature. That afternoon I had gone to be by myself for a while, when I saw a thunderstorm piling up. When it broke, there I was, sitting on a big rock—and right in the middle of it, with the thunder bursting and the wind whistling, it came to me that what I had to do was take pictures and concentrate upon people, only people, all kinds of people, people who paid me and people who didn't.

It was not until 1932 that such a vision helped give birth to one of the enduring images of photographic history. Late that year, the Depression had descended upon the country in unalleviated force. The poor and the hungry milled about the streets of San Francisco. Near Lange's studio a wealthy matron known as the "White Angel" had set up a bread line, and the photographer, glancing out the window, watched the cluster of hopeless men waiting for a handout. Worried about the possibility of resentment, even violence, she asked her brother, Martin, who had relocated to the city, to join her as she ventured from the safe confines of the studio with her camera. But the forlorn people in the streets had other things, perhaps only misery, on their minds. She approached the group and started taking pictures of defeated men huddled in their winter coats. Remembering the experience later, she said: "I knew I was looking at something. You know there are moments such as these when time

Workers Unite, San Francisco, 1934

San Francisco, 1934

stands still and all you do is hold your breath and hope it will wait for you. . . . You know that you are not taking anything away from anyone: their privacy, their dignity, their wholeness."

In the months that followed, she left her studio at every opportunity and wandered the city's streets. She posted announcements of small, invitation-only showings of her "pictures of people," then "photographs of people"—not the wealthy sitters, but individuals she was discovering in streets, in demonstrations, men and women trailing into the city from blighted states across the union. She had even come across a motto that William Carlos Williams would have understood right down to his bone marrow: "The contemplation of things as they are, without substitution or imposture, without error or confusion, is in itself a nobler thing than a whole harvest of invention." Francis Bacon wrote the words centuries ago; Lange kept them posted on her studio door. For a photographer they amount to a more controversial message than a quick, pietistic reading might suggest.

The picture offers the "contemplation" of a "thereness," which such existentialist philosophers as Martin Heidegger or Gabriel Marcel make so much of—and yet, inevitably, a degree of "invention" takes place. Who is imposing (with how much claim to truth, with how much substitution or imposture) on what particular scene? Such a question began occurring to Dorothea Lange at just the point she embarked on a career as a documentary photographer—and the asking was a measure of a continuing sensitivity and thoughtfulness.

She began to show pictures, but as yet received no critical response, no open-armed acceptance by the budding community of West Coast art photographers. The fall of 1932 marked the founding of the Group f/64, a potent if brief movement in photography devoted to the "straight print." The original group included Ansel Adams, Edward Weston, Imogen Cunningham, Henry F. Swift, John Paul Edwards, and Willard Van Dyke. Lange knew them, knew they held informal discussions, but never volunteered nor was asked to join. She was not then, not until the end of her life, ready to consider her work as "art," and her interests led her into the streets, not into coteries. Yet, in 1934, five of Lange's prints appeared in *Camera Craft,* accompanied by a critical estimate by Van Dyke that remains, perhaps, the best appraisal of her work. She had just embarked upon the documentary phase of her career, so the text seems particularly prophetic:

Dorothea Lange has turned to the people of the American scene with the intention of making an adequate photographic record of them. These people are in the midst of great changes–contemporary problems are reflected on their faces, a tremendous drama is unfolding before them, and Dorothea Lange is photographing it through them.

She sees the final criticism of her work in the reaction to it of some person who might view it fifty years from now. It is her hope that such a person would see in her work a record of the people of her time, a record valid of the day and place wherein made, although necessarily incomplete in the sense of the entire contemporary movement. . . .

Miss Lange's work is motivated by no preconceived photographic aesthetic. Her attitude bears a significant analogy to the sensitized plate of the camera itself. For her, making a shot is an adventure that begins with no planned itinerary. She feels that setting out with a preconceived idea of

Howard Street, San Francisco, 1934

what she wants to photograph actually minimizes her chance for success. Her method is to eradicate from her mind before she starts, all ideas which she might hold regarding the situation–her mind like an unexposed film.

In an old Ford she drives to a place most likely to yield subjects consistent with her general sympathies. Unlike the newspaper reporter, she has no news or editorial policies to direct her movements; it is only her deeply personal sympathies for the unfortunate, the downtrodden, the misfits, among her contemporaries that provide the impetus for her expedition. She may park her car at the waterfront during a strike, perhaps at a meeting of unemployed, by sleepers in the city square, at transient shelters–bread lines, parades, or demonstrations. Here she waits with her camera open and unconcealed, her mind ready.

What is she seeking–what is the essence of the human situation and through what elements or items does it reveal itself? The scene is a panorama, constantly shifting and rearranging. For her it is transformed into a pageant of humanity across the ground glass–the drama moves, the individuals stir and mill about, by what motivation she cares little. It may be hours before a climax arrives worthy of the decisive click of the shutter. Suddenly out of the chaos of disorganized movement, the ground glass becomes alive, not in the human sense alone, but in the sense that only a photographer can recognize–a scene, a negative, finally a print that is itself alive. . . .

There is no attempt made to conceal her apparatus, Miss Lange merely appears to take as little interest in the proceedings around her as is possible. She looks at no individual directly, and soon she becomes one of the familiar elements of her surroundings. Her subjects become unaware of her presence. Her method, as she describes it, is to act as if she possessed the power to become invisible to those around her. This mental attitude enables her to completely ignore those who might resent her presence.

Perhaps we can arrive at a better evaluation of her record in terms of a future observer than as contemporary critics. We ourselves are too poignantly involved in the turmoil of present life. Much of it is stupid, confused, violent, some little of it is significant, all of it is of the most immediate concern to everyone living today–we have no time for the records, ourselves living and dying in the recording.

We can assume the role of that future critic by looking back to the work of Mathew Brady, who in the dawn of photography made a heroic record of another crisis in American life. Brady and Lange have both made significant use of their common medium–they differ mainly in terms of the tech-

Dorothea Lange photographing at a California migrant camp, 1937 (Rondal Partridge)

Dorothea Lange and Paul Taylor on field trip, 1935 (Helen Dixon)

nical advancement of the medium itself. Lange can photograph the split-seconds of the dynamic surges of the scene about her–Brady, carrying a complete darkroom about with him through the northern battlefields of the Civil War, sensitizing his own plates before each shot, making twenty-minute exposures, had to wait for the ample lulls between engagements. The implications of his record are retrospective, the scene after the battle, the dead that were once living, the ruins that were once forts, faces still and relaxed. Both Lange and Brady share the passionate desire to show posterity the mixture of futility and hope, of heroism and stupidity, greatness and banality that are the concomitants of man's struggle forward.

It was also Van Dyke's exhibition that brought Dorothea together with Paul Taylor, economist from the University of California. His interests, energies, concerns connected so powerfully to her artistic life that one has a hard time imagining Dorothea Lange's career without Taylor—even as her work gave an enormous lift to his aspirations as a socially-minded economist, a compassionate activist.

Paul Taylor came to California from Iowa, had studied at the University of Wisconsin, had become, early on, a committed populist. He became interested in the problems of Mexican migrant workers during the 1920s, well before the Great Depression, well before white families from the drought-struck Midwest would, in their hard, if not desperate travels, add a new dimension to what abstractly gets called the question of migratory labor.

In Mexico he observed the world left behind by so many agricultural workers—the poverty, the mix of Indian and Spanish culture, the necessary but reluctant departure (lest virtual starvation take place) north to California, Arizona, Texas and points beyond. As he amassed his statistics, conducted his interviews, he found himself wanting to record what he saw. He took snapshots, lots of them. He was trying to capture evidence, rather than take "interesting" pictures. He was a social scientist with a strong conscience, not a photographer anxious to respond artistically, dramatically to a given scene. An article by Taylor on the migrant labor problem of the American Southwest was published in *Survey Graphic* in 1931. The editor, Paul Kellogg, commissioned Ansel Adams to take some photographs to accompany the text. Kellogg had previously hired Lewis Hine for the same purpose—to provide readers with visual referents for words, numbers, and percentages. Lange and Taylor would accomplish something different, something more.

Their first short project together was a study of self-help cooperatives organized to deal with local economic emergencies. In the course of their work together, as he interviewed and gathered data and she photographed the apparently hopeless but valiant efforts of sawmill workers, Lange and Taylor drew close, fell in love. Her marriage to Dixon had entered its final stages: ill, still painting but feeble, nearing sixty, Dixon's one ambition was to return to Taos. Taylor, too, was in the process of obtaining a divorce. The separated couples remained amicable and on December 6, 1935, Taylor and Lange married. In daily life, in work, they would remain virtually inseparable until her death. She once confided to an interviewer, describing her marriage to Dixon, "I wasn't really involved in the vitals of the man, not in the vitals." With Taylor, the union was complete, and together they entered into a period of great accomplishment.

Dorothea Lange, 1936 (Rondal Partridge)

Looking back, the Farm Security Administration (FSA) photography seems like an unlikely, utterly fortunate accident. It emerged in the heady shuffle and reshuffle of government agencies as Franklin D. Roosevelt's New Deal plunged into the task of reviving a shattered economy. Organized under Roy E. Stryker, who also was a relatively unlikely yet happy choice, the FSA Historical Section, as it was formally known, managed to amass more than 250,000 negatives in seven years—an unparalleled chronicle of national change. Far more important, these images were the work of masters, though hardly recognized as such at the time. Walker Evans, Russell Lee, Arthur Rothstein, Ben Shahn, and, of course, Dorothea Lange were among the less than a dozen photographers employed by Stryker, some for only a few months.

After their first expedition together, Taylor managed to have Lange hired as a photographer while he investigated problems of the migrant workers pouring into California. The Relief Administration had never had a photographer connected to its studies. Finally, an imaginative office manager agreed: she was officially designated Taylor's "typist"; her photographic materials were purchased under the budget line item "office supplies"; and she was given a one-month trial period.

In February 1935, Lange accompanied Taylor and his team on trips to study migrants harvesting in Nipomo and in the Imperial Valley. She had watched him carefully before—his easy, conversational style of coaxing hard data out of the most generalized interview. On the first day, she, too, chatted easily with the destitute migrants, asking about their work, where they came from, their children. Toilets were holes dug in the ground; there was no clean water supply. Work was occasional. Disease and malnutrition showed starkly upon faces of men, women, and children. Lange took pictures, listened, and quickly jotted down the remarks. Taylor was pleased, perhaps surprised. Her field notes figured prominently among the data gathered by his own "trained" assistants from the university, and they were pithy, revealing: "We got blowed out of Oklahoma." "It seems like God has forsaken us back there in Arkansas."

After the trip, Lange helped organize the report, edited and laid out photographs, bound pages. The result was the first appropriation, $20,000, to establish a migrant's camp. It opened in Marysville, California, in October, and set the pattern for a score more. Lange's pictures also won space in newspapers, and the vital editorial support relief efforts needed to overcome—even at the beginning—stormy resistance from the growers' associations.

Taylor's next assignment was with the Federal Emergency Relief Agency (FERA), which had funded the Marysville camp and subsequent settlements. At first, the direct employer was called the Rural Rehabilitation Division, which

Migratory Worker's Kitchen, near Shafter, California, November 1936

Family near Sacramento, May 1935

quickly acquired another bureaucratic niche and name, the Relief Administration, ultimately to be called the Farm Security Administration. At its head was a bold and brilliant economist from Columbia University, Rexford Guy Tugwell—a member of Roosevelt's "Brain Trust," and an anathema to corporate agriculture and conservatives, who decried the "socialist" impulse behind government efforts to help the poor. Tugwell had worked with Stryker, another Columbia economist, whose writings and lectures had effectively used photographs to communicate the facts and theories of their discipline. Tugwell knew that his relief efforts demanded powerful support to survive opposition—both in the highest reaches of government and at the grass roots level across the nation. A battle of heart, mind, and conscience was inevitable.

Such political developments enlarged the Taylor-Lange orbit beyond California to include Arizona, Nevada, New Mexico, and Utah. Their initial report had created a stir, finding its way into the hands of Eleanor Roosevelt, Secretary of Agriculture Henry A. Wallace, and Secretary of the Interior Harold Ickes. Stryker personally counted among his own qualifications no great knowledge of photography; he had no bias about "schools," "approaches," or "art" versus "document." He needed pictures that showed the greatness of the need, and also the progress of the Tugwell-administered relief efforts. Lange's pictures told a story and appealed to the editors and readers of national publications. He brought her into his still somewhat confused operation with its miniscule budget, uncertain plans. Working hit-and-miss, he had discovered an often rambunctious collection of superb talents. Soon, he realized that the FSA had a special gift for recording a chapter of turmoil—heroic response to turmoil—in the country's history.

All this occurred just as Taylor and Lange prepared to marry. It was a tumultuous period. The challenges of their work filled them with exhilaration. At home, they had a no less difficult task—merging a family that included her two sons by Dixon and Taylor's three children by his former marriage. She and Stryker had already embarked on a voluminous, revealing correspond-

North Beach District, San Francisco, 1936

Lunchtime for Peach Pickers, Musella, Georgia, 1936

ence. Her first request was for the funds to purchase equipment, lenses, supplies. He responded by citing the financial restraints that marked the usually hard-pressed FSA, advising her to rent a darkroom—then wait for equipment. The first assignment took her back to Marysville, where she made pictures of Tom Collins, the camp manager who was the model for the manager in John Steinbeck's *The Grapes of Wrath.*

Anxious to be at work, she and Taylor turned their Albuquerque wedding into a working honeymoon. In the afternoon following the ceremony, she went out to photograph. Ambitious expeditions were planned, then canceled for lack of funds. She photographed locally—pea pickers, the devastation of soil erosion.

The early weeks were filled with frustrations for Lange, indecision in Washington. She paid for the first field trips out of her own pocket, and applied for reimbursement. On her first major trip alone in spring 1936, she shot the image that would win a place in newspapers throughout the world and established without doubt the moving, persuasive power of a photograph.

She had been on the road for a month. She had traveled up to fourteen hours a day, photographing, keeping the meticulous records demanded by Washington—of mileage, pennies spent, and exposures made. She had been working over field notes, cleaning and worrying about her equipment. She was returning home on a rainy, cold, miserable March evening. A sign, "PEA-PICKERS CAMP," caught her eye near Nipomo, and she ignored it. Her work was done on that trip, and done well. She drove on for another twenty miles, and, as she later recalled, the question kept recurring in her mind, "Are you going back?" She fought it, even as she wheeled the car around, retraced the twenty miles, drove off the road and into a soggy, forlorn collection of tents. An exhausted mother sitting with her children in a tent caught her eye. Lange spent less than ten minutes with the woman, making five exposures, learning that the crop had frozen, the woman and children were living on vegetables scavenged from the fields, and the few birds the children managed to catch. The mother could not leave; she had sold the tires from her car.

One of those exposures, titled *Migrant Mother,* became the best-known photograph made by Stryker's group, one of the most widely reproduced and exhibited images in history. Many years later, writing the introductory essay for the Lange retrospective in The Museum of Modern Art, George P. Elliott grasped, as few have, the magic of such a photograph:

"Migrant Mother" is famous because key people, editors and so on, themselves finding it inexhaustibly rich, have urged the rest of the world to look at it. This picture, like a few others of a few other photographers, leads a life of its own. That is, it is widely accepted as a work of art with its own message rather than its maker's; far more people know the picture than know who made it. There is a sense in which a photographer's apotheosis is to become as anonymous as his camera. For an artist like Dorothea Lange who does not primarily aim to make photographs that are ends in themselves, the making of a great, perfect, anonymous photograph is a trick of grace, about which she can do little beyond making herself available for that gift of grace.

How reluctantly she had turned around, had headed back to the camp! The picture would never be unequivocally gratifying for Lange. For years she grumbled that it had threatened to make her known as a one-picture photographer.

In the summer of 1936 Taylor and Lange were briefly assigned to Washington. Now their coverage of the dislocations and distress of America's small landholders, its yeomen, its landless

Migrant Mother, Nipomo, California, 1936

rural laborers would acquire the breadth and profundity of the entire national experience. She roamed with camera toward the East, into the South, through the Carolinas, across Mississippi and Alabama.

With or without Taylor, her way of working remained simple, direct, friendly—and honest. She approached a farmhouse, a field, men lounging on the porch of a general store. She struck up conversations easily and to the point: What chores were being performed? What had the weather been like recently? Were crop prices rising or falling? The answers told her about what people knew—their skills at planting, plowing, cooking. She learned how much money her informants had, what their prospects were. Quickly they grew accustomed to the short, interested woman, perhaps a little outlandish in her slacks, a beret covering her short-cut hair. She asked if she might take pictures and pulled out the two cameras—the Rolleiflex, the 4 x 5 Graflex. She let the children look at the cameras, handle them (something that drove her to fury at home, when her own children touched, sometimes broke her equipment). She seldom shot indoors, seldom used artificial light. But she used everything else she had—including her lameness. No matter that she arrived in a car, worked for the government. The limp showed that she, too, knew the unfairness of life; and she was on their side, wanted to tell their story, wanted to help.

Lange prided herself on never taking a picture of anyone who objected. If she was told not to photograph, she put the cameras away, talked to people, asked again. If they still refused, she drove off. If an individual edged away or hid from the camera, her curiosity was always aroused. Perhaps that was the one, the story, the image. Still, she would not push too hard; she would not override the reluctance of the unwilling. Nor would she aim her lenses at scenes of great emotional stress. Such moments of crisis, she always felt, belonged to the person.

Lange's methods usually worked rather well—though they were tested most during her FSA trips in the deep South. Here she was not among the uprooted, the wanderers, as she had been in California. The scenes along the Delta, in plantations, in small "general-store" hamlets, were of people still bound by long, unbroken tradition. Here her intentions could be, and often were, suspect. She had no time for embarrassment, let alone fear. Yet the characteristic difficulties and doubts of her work must have plagued her, never so eloquently expressed, I think, as in the recollections of Lillian Smith. This white southern woman, a writer, vividly portrayed what

Migrant Mother, Nipomo, California, 1936

Migrant Mother, Nipomo, California, 1936

it was like in the 1930s and early 1940s to stake out an intellectual and political course, and to travel on its behalf. The author of *Strange Fruit* and *One Hour*, once wrote to me:

I would move about Georgia, talking with people and listening to them. I was a writer, of course, a journalist. I wanted to know what was happening in my native region. I wanted to know how the poor were living. I worried about the Negro people; my heart went out to them. I even tried to go up to them and have a decent, intelligent conversation with them—not some farce of a talk, some make-believe talk, in which no one says anything serious, and no one looks anyone in the eye. But to break through, to cross the color line, to cross the sex line–these were considered outrageous steps, especially in the rural part of the South.

I learned to play one taboo against the other, though. I could make mistakes that no white man *would dare make; I was a woman, after all, and so one to be pampered or tolerated or smiled at, but not taken seriously! On the other hand, as a woman, a white woman, I was constantly being stared at, and I had to deal with the surprise, the suspiciousness and resentment of a lot of people—men and women, Negroes and whites. The poor, the poor Negroes—lots of them thought I was a loony woman! What in the world did I want to know from them—about them? Who in the world was I? Why in the world was I spending my good, God-given time moving about and looking at people in trouble and talking with them? After awhile, I began to ask* myself *those questions! I think if you are doing something the society doesn't like, you begin to wear down; you begin to think of the world the way your worst critics, your out-and-out enemies think of the world. They're ready to jump you, and so you keep yourself braced for the assault, and the result is they've won without that assault. After I'd been on the road long enough, I had all those distrustful or hostile glances in front of my mind, even if I actually missed seeing them; and I was always wondering myself why I was poking around—even if I got angry with myself, pronto, and went about my business. It was a tough time the country was going through, and no one very important in Georgia wanted some nosy lady picking up lids here and there, and looking to see what was inside all the cans.*

Lange, too, was a quiet, unprepossessing American woman. Yet, if all was calm in the so-called anthropological field, the relationship between Stryker and Lange was a dizzying mix of quarrels and admiration. He knew well the value of her work to the FSA, to the Administration's relief efforts. A vastly disproportionate share of the requests for illustrations—to accompany Congressional reports, newspaper and magazine articles, books and pamphlets, and to appear in exhibitions and, increasingly, in museums—were for the work of Dorothea Lange. Stryker was most anxious to place pictures in such magazines as *Life* and *Look*, rapidly becoming the most widely

Waiting for Relief Checks, Calipatria, California, 1937

Rural Oklahoma, 1938

read publications in the country. Lange's photographs most often interested the editors.

Lange and Stryker also shared an appreciation of the history they chronicled, and, perhaps, were shaping. Each knew that the story of a migrant camp, a displaced tenant farmer, a Texas drought, belonged inextricably to the mosaic of event and change stretching from coast to coast. She also had another virtue in Stryker's eyes—her assiduous note taking and terse, information-filled captions.

The FSA chief carped constantly at Russell Lee, Arthur Rothstein, and other staff photographers about the inadequacy and careless redundancy of their accompanying captions. Lange, working alongside a talented social scientist, valued the words that went with the pictures, that let the people in her prints tell *their* story, in *their* words. She had an extraordinary ear for the revealing detail, for dialect. Along with the photographs of six displaced tenant farmers in Hardeman County, Texas, made in 1936, she sent the following information: the men were all under thirty-five, each supported an average family of four on $22.80 a month in Works Progress Administration relief. "The landlord on this place bought a tractor and put five families of renters off. He has two families on day labor, at from 75 cents to $1.25 a day." None of them could vote—they couldn't afford the Texas poll tax. They couldn't change things, didn't even know who the enemy was. As one put it, "If we fight, who we gonna whup?"

Lange's commitment to the division was without qualification. Many years later, she was to say, "Once an FSA guy, always an FSA guy." It was a unique time, a unique group. She enjoyed the near chaotic office in Washington, reveled in the friendly welcome that greeted her when she made her infrequent trips to headquarters. She liked Stryker, responded with care to his sometimes detailed suggestions, and exchanged ideas for projects. She did her homework—reading speeches by Administration officials, government reports, studies by sociologists and economists. These researches always followed her shooting expeditions, when she edited and selected photographs, and wrote captions that often included excerpts from her reading. She possessed, as one friend described it, a "pell mell enthusiasm" for her work—once traveling 17,000 grueling miles on an assignment.

Against this background, though, she and Stryker headed toward a serious rift. They might have esteemed each other, but each was opinionated and disagreeable when crossed. Her letters abound with complaints and demands. When advances and back pay were not forthcoming on time, she spent her own money on equipment,

Dorothea Lange, 1934

Tenant Farmers, Hardeman County, Texas, June 1937

supplies, water and electricity, assistants, making Stryker—who was himself battling penny by penny for his division—feel guilty. They argued and he often found her presence in Washington disruptive—even paralyzing.

The crucial argument throughout her tenure with FSA was over possession of negatives. In her letters she constantly pleaded to keep them in California, where she could work on them, supervise printing and selection. He sympathized, especially when she pointed out that the western regional offices and newspapers had special needs to combat reactionary groups trying to thwart FSA programs. The greater need, though, was in Washington, he retorted—the center through which requests from all over the nation passed.

Still, she resisted, and her stubbornness hints at an underlying insecurity—beyond the understandable desire of any photographer to keep possession of negatives. Lange was never a brilliant, perhaps not even a good, technician. Her correspondence to Stryker is filled with advance apologies: that equipment had failed (as hers often did); that heat, cold, damp might have spoiled negatives. She requested, sometimes with success, that her friend Ansel Adams be allowed to develop negatives, make prints. It was a wise choice. Intrinsic to the beauty of Adams's photographs is a carefully evolved craftsmanship perhaps never equaled in photography. He is both a master and innovator of technique. Lange viewed the darkroom with terror, knew the labor required to upgrade her sometimes poorly exposed negatives to good prints. She knew she possessed an eye for reading a negative, for understanding its possibilities. Even more, she knew where the compelling emotional resonance of the print lay.

When Adams could not be turned to, she directed her assistants with specific detail, left the accomplishment of the task to them. In the darkroom and on the road, her favorite assistant-technician in the FSA period was Rondal Partridge, the teen-age son of Imogen Cunningham and Roi. Subsequent helpers attest to her disinterest in technique, her errors in choosing film, paper.

Stryker tried to compromise by sending her all the negatives she requested, with the provision she return them after the prints were made—a provision Lange always procrastinated about fulfilling. Stryker later recalled, "We practically had to send the sheriff to get them back for the files." One source of her reluctance was Stryker's habit of rejecting negatives by perforating them with two neat, utterly destructive holes. Walker Evans is said to have been infuriated to the point of near madness by the vandalism. He, Lange, and perhaps others, responded at times by withholding the one negative they liked best of several exposures.

Such quarrels began to erode the Stryker-Lange relationship, more seriously, perhaps, than she knew. In 1938 and 1939 she was on and off the official payroll: sometimes on a *per diem* basis, sometimes paid by negative—three dollars for each accepted! Stryker's fury reached a peak, however, when he learned that she had hired Ansel Adams to print and mount several pictures—from negatives he had lent back—for a show at The Museum of Modern Art in New York. He was even more enraged that she had hired an expert retoucher to correct flaws on the negatives, including that of *Migrant Mother.* Stryker constantly watchdogged his photographers to make sure they didn't get trapped in "art"—didn't succumb to the "preciousness" of it. He wanted pictures that told the story. There was no objection at FSA to posed photographs, but he was adamant about the purity of negatives.

Lange explained, tried to smooth things over, to no avail. Late in 1939 she was informed, rath-

Ex-tenant Farmer on Relief Grant, Imperial Valley, California, 1937

er curtly, that her employment by FSA would be officially and finally terminated at the beginning of 1940. Lange and Taylor were both deeply hurt, especially by Stryker's refusal to authorize a final small payment for the cleaning and repair of her cameras. Friends tried to heal the breach; one of them, Jonathan Garst of the regional FSA office, wrote to his chief, reminding him of the couple's great contribution to their work. Moreover, Garst wrote, "Paul Taylor is still violently in love with Dorothea Lange and takes her problems very much to heart. As a matter of fact, I think anything that would hurt her feelings would have very much more effect on Paul's feelings than anything that was done to him directly."

Stryker remained unmoved. He believed that Lange's reputation would easily gain her assignments from the picture magazines and from other government agencies. She completed her last captions and sent to Washington the negatives of her final expedition. For years bitterness lingered between Stryker and Lange. Ultimately, the shared experiences, the remembrance of better times, led them back to a warmer, easier friendship. Still, even in the midst of his anger at Lange, Stryker retained a sense of fair play; he continued to dispatch to Lange and Taylor the negatives for their book *An American Exodus,* which was published in 1939.

Though it found a favorable critical audience, *An American Exodus* was virtually ignored by a public caught up in a different national mood. The war had been unleashed in Europe; America was re-arming. Employment increased, at first slowly, then explosively. The historic period that Taylor and Lange had so profoundly conveyed was swept from the nation's mind by the new, even greater drama of a world at war.

Dorothea Lange's accomplishments during those five short years with the FSA are so evident today, so much a part of our national consciousness of the era, that we may well lose sight of how original her contribution was. Her photographs marshaled public sympathy for a necessary relief program. Her photographs persuaded a reluctant Congressional committee to vote funds for that program. Those photographs were part of what is called the documentary tradition. Lange did not need such terms, though; she simply wanted to see and hear, to render and evoke, to transmit, arouse, and record. Yet documentary work, whether visual or written, skirts dangerous

Family on the Road, Oklahoma, 1938

Farmers at Tobacco Auction, Douglas, Georgia, 1938

edges of misunderstanding and misuse. Always there is the question of motive, of purpose. What were Lange and Taylor really trying to do? What were their aims? The most direct answer is: they were trying to create social and political change. Such a goal, of course, aroused strong criticism from unanticipated, as well as expected, quarters.

When my wife and I talked with Taylor (he was well over eighty) in the Berkeley home he shared for so long with Dorothea Lange, he could still remember the response of any number of his fellow social scientists to the collaborative work he did with his wife. Photographs are "irrelevant," or worse, "subjective," even "inflammatory," he was told. The proper perspective is dispassionate, detached analysis—as opposed to polemical statement, propaganda. Nor would Dorothea Lange be allowed to pursue her intellectual and moral instincts, her particular inclinations as an artist, without a similar kind of reaction from certain colleagues—art demeaned, art as an instrument of indoctrination, of partisan ideological persuasion.

Not all photographers (and not necessarily out of selfishness or heartless indifference) liked the idea of their colleagues spending time and federal money in a constant search for only one side of American life—the "human erosion" Dorothea Lange and Paul Taylor mention in *An American Exodus*. But the book is explicitly meant to be a "record" of that erosion, and by inference, a call for action.

Spring Plowing, Cauliflower Fields, Guadalupe, California, 1937

The intention, as a work of social science, is unmistakably on the table—to show the waste, the cheapness and meanness of life in the South, in the central states, in our West. Lange and Taylor offered a predominantly visual kind of social geography. The titles of the sections go from east to west—the exodus, but also, the historical referents of the American experience: Old South, Plantation under the Machine; Mid-Continent; Plains; Dirt Bowl; and, finally, Lost West. We wince now, aware that there are, clearly, other Wests—the kin of the individuals whom Dorothea Lange portrays, once "Okies," live in Southern California quite comfortably. Ironically many of them have strong conservative convictions—shun any scheme to reawaken a concern for any "human erosion" that may now be taking place.

As social investigators, Lange and Taylor followed a remarkable tradition nurtured at Chapel Hill's University of North Carolina, during the 1920s and 1930s. It is no accident that Rupert Vance is quoted several times in *An American Exodus*. Vance and Howard Odum and their colleagues were social scientists who had no infatuation with jargon; they were a different breed of social scientist, the kind who favored clear, pungent prose mobilized to the purposes of direct, careful observation, with theoretical speculation kept under watchful tether. They had every interest in reaching a broad public, readers of general magazines and newspapers, in hopes that obvious inequities, not to mention injustices, would be addressed. Moreover, the North Carolina social scientists were unashamedly subjective and without hesitation announced their moral positions. They abandoned even the pretense of being "value-free" and they never tried for a language that announced neutrality or emphasized the secret, guarded world of the academy. Lange and Taylor used a phrase Vance used, in the middle 1930s, to describe the Mississippi Delta: "Negro-obsessed."

Vance knew, however, and made sure his readers knew, that obsessions come and go. The "Negro-obsessed" Delta now has integrated schools more successfully than has Boston, despite its abolitionist history. Those who know that history hasten to point out the reason—remind us that a good number of abolitionists were "Irish-obsessed," while favoring emancipation and more for distant blacks. Still, ambiguity can be found outside of New England, too—even in the Delta of the 1930s. A black sharecropper once described for me the period and its aftermath:

There was a lot of hate when I was a young man, in 1925 and 1930 and 1935. You bet. There was hate in Europe and hate in America all over—race riots in the northern cities, I recall. We had hate down here; we had lynchings in Mississippi. I'm not one to sit back and tell you the white people and the black people loved each other back then, or do now, either. But we had a lot we went through together. We suffered a lot, no matter the person's race. We helped each other a lot. We weren't the equal of the white, no question. But we had white friends. We had white neighbors who'd talk real friendly to you, and they'd take you to the doctor, and they'd send over food. I know, I know—it wasn't like it should be. But I went North. I tried Chicago. It was worse up there. No white man would say hello. No white man would give you the time of day. They got violent up there, and invaded our streets, and killed our people. I came back to Mississippi.

My son has gone to college up North. He's read the books and he's heard the lectures—about us black southern folk. He says they don't get it right. He says he picks up a book, and it says that Mississippi is a bad place, full of racists. True, we have them! But we have a lot of other people here, too.

When the Civil Rights people came here, I was glad. I'm not telling the world that I favor the Klan, or the old kind of sheriffs we used to have. I'm just saying that even then, when we had a lot of trouble—well, there was a lot of trouble all over. And I felt back then, during the 1960s, even though I gave my home over to the students, who were fighting the cause of Civil Rights—I felt that you have to be careful about what you say about this *town or* this *state, or* that *town or* that *state; and you have to be careful when you take your pictures, too. They were always running here and there with their cameras. They wanted to send pictures back home, to their families up North—showing how bad we have it down here, and we didn't have indoor plumbing, and all that. My*

Cotton Sharecroppers, Greene County, Georgia, 1937

Hoeing, near Yazoo City, Mississippi, 1937

Wife of a Cotton Farmer, Greene County, Georgia, 1937

wife got upset, and so did I. I'll tell you why: we're not doing as good as we should be doing, that's for sure, but we're not as low and no count a people as some would tell the world. We have our good times. We can wear a smile on our faces, and mean it.

Once I heard some of the SNCC people [Student Nonviolent Coordinating Committee, a Civil Rights group of the early 1960s] saying we're the "poorest of the poor," they said, and we're "victims," and we're "on the bottom of the ladder." I told them they'd better look again—and again. I told them they're looking for what they've already seen but they aren't looking to see the whole truth for themselves. They asked me what *they should go see. I reminded them of their own words. Didn't they tell me the other day how much they like staying with us, and how "good" we are, and how they'd like to stay here forever, because we're "the finest people in the world!" They said yes. But they still didn't know what I was getting at. So, I told them that you can't have it both ways. Either we're good, and that means it's not all bad here, or we're truly bad, and then we can't be complimented all the time for being so courageous, and having such nice families, and treating our kids so nice, and all the other things we've been told we do!*

A person who could be called poor and illiterate and an extremely marginal member of our social and economic system turns out to be, also, a shrewd observer of others, a keen analyst of certain social and psychological matters, a fine logician—able to spot inconsistencies and spell them out. His observations do not obliterate the terrible facts of poverty—as they were in the 1930s and as they continue to be in the 1980s—and neither do they invalidate the moral and political indignation of *An American Exodus*, of the FSA photo-documentary tradition, and of similar studies. The call of sympathy, empathy—yes, to political activism—was a reasonable one fifty years ago, and still is today. A photographer has every right to heed a particular expedition's imperatives: show the hurt and sorrow; show the waste of human resources; show the plain scandal of people treated unjustly, meanly by other people.

The issue is not one of accuracy as against distortion—at least of the deliberate, mischievous variety. The black people who figure in *An American Exodus* are extremely hard-pressed men and women, and their misery is no fictive matter, no mirage conjured by a camera at the beck and call of a Washington, D.C., bureaucrat, anxious to stay on the federal payroll. The same goes for the

FSA Loan Recipient, Malheur County, Oregon, 1938

Elm Grove, Oklahoma, c. 1938

Oklahoma and Texas farm and small-town people whom Lange caught (I believe) in all their complex relationship to the Midwestern land, never a completely reliable provider, due to the unpredictability of the weather. In the best of her pictures, individuals appear harrassed, yet determined; humbled, yet proud; uncertain, yet quite clear about what series of misfortunes have happened, what (hope against hope) must happen, if complete disaster is to be avoided. In other words, life's contradictions and inconsistencies, so acutely perceived by the black Mississippi sharecropper, have a way of demanding their due, no matter the particular, honorable intent of an observer who was quite properly horrified at the sight of human loss, at the sight of a community's "erosion"; and who was anxious to portray such a development so that others would know and be inclined to act.

Nevertheless, a "record" is commonly less clear-cut than some of us observers might wish. The best tribute an outsider who comes, watches or listens, then abruptly leaves, can offer the victim is some acknowledgment of the strain of negotiating an exceedingly difficult apologia. In the words of a Delta farmhand:

We want help. We need a lot of help. But we don't want to be looked down on, and called a new bunch of names, to replace the old ones. I'd rather be someone's son-of-a-bitch, than someone's beaten down goner, about to disappear from the face of the earth! I'd rather be neither; I'd rather be myself, only better off. How do you get better off? And when you are better off, how do you get to be "yourself," and no copy-cat of everyone else?

Not a bad kind of existentialist questioning. Not a bad kind of human observation—and self-scrutiny. Not a bad mandate for the rest of us—to remember the divergent aspects of subjectivity and objectivity alike, as we compile our various "records," state our "conclusions." I suspect that many who have had Dorothea Lange's level of moral earnestness have succeeded not necessarily because of, but often enough, in spite of, the presence of that particular quality of mind and heart. Certainly *An American Exodus* is more than a tale of woe. Some of the photographs show desolation; show a collapsing agricultural order; show perplexity or a contained but unmistakable resentment. But even those black and white representations of human reality turn out to be—just that: inescapably ambiguous, in keeping with the strange contradictions of this life.

The problem of preconception, of intent, is paramount to the worker. When my wife and I started going from home to home in Louisiana,

Revival Meeting in a Garage, Dos Palos, California, 1938

Shacktown, Elm Grove, Oklahoma, 1936

Mississippi, Alabama, and Georgia in the late 1950s and early 1960s, an issue rose between us about my point of view. I was a child psychiatrist, I was undergoing psychoanalysis (in New Orleans, where we lived) and was beginning psychoanalytic training, and my job was to find out what the serious stress of school desegregation (then beginning, with terrible riots the result) did to the minds of the children and families caught up in the continuing turmoil—a moment of historic change if there ever was one! The point was to listen, detect what one mind, then another, was doing, then fit the various responses into categories—the "mechanisms of defense" that the mind uses to deal with inner and outer psychological demands. We worked conscientiously at that for awhile, but after a month or so my wife became annoyed with me as I pointed out a "denial" here, a "reaction-formation" there. She eventually told me something that I would never forget: "You are always *characterizing* the people we see! Why don't you let them *be*? Why don't you pay attention to each person in each family we visit, and stop trying to lump them together—first one way, then another!"

We had reached an impasse, because she would continue giving me that message, and I would get up on my high professional horse and announce what I knew, and what I was trained to do, and what the nature of psychiatric research required. In return I received a blast or two: forget "methodology" and even "research," and keep listening and asking questions—and yes, God forbid, relax more, stop being so insistently eager to come up with answers. Moreover, she insisted again and again, each child, each family, is different. Why not start out by recognizing *that,* and even documenting the varieties of difference? Why not try to get to the heart of the matter in one home, then another—and let the "defense mechanisms" and the "attitudes" and the answers to specific questions take care of themselves?

Even if I hadn't been thereby brought back to sanity, I think I would have had to stop and think again about what I was trying to do in the South, because I was gradually becoming overwhelmed by an astonishing variation in thought and feeling, in opinion and sentiment, in asserted loyalties or preferences, and in asserted dislikes or outright antagonisms. And not only among the black families we'd set out to get to know, but the white people who were, virtually, carrying on a war (certainly with respect to their emotions) against the federal government. If blacks had been stereotyped for years as "lazy" or "apathetic" or "dumb" (Stepin Fetchit and Amos 'n' Andy and on and on), southern whites had not exactly been lionized by America's liberal intellectuals, for whom (and I must reluctantly mention myself and a good number of other Yankees associated with the Civil Rights movement) a white tenant farmer, say, or a small-town clerk, was likely to be considered, without question, a

Crossroads Store, Rural Georgia, 1938

Plantation Worker, Memphis, Tennessee, 1938

"redneck," a "cracker," a probable member of some Klan or White Citizen's Council, and surely a "racist."

When we first started talking with the white members of a New Orleans mob that heckled, every day, the sole black child, Ruby, who was integrating (*sic!*) a totally boycotted elementary school (William Frantz), it is not hard to imagine all the "defense mechanisms" easily picked up and later tabulated in the wake of conversations: paranoiac projections, displacements, introjections. Colleagues asked me constantly what was *wrong* with "those people"—what kind of Americans were they? Surely they belonged in mental hospitals. Surely they were severely "disturbed"—the constant outpouring of hate at a six-year-old girl. Surely something troublesome in their own lives had engaged with this social and political incident. Surely a "normal" person would not take to the streets and threaten a child—and keep his or her own child out of a school because one black girl had been observed to attend it. Among those who had such a viewpoint were psychiatrists from the North as well as those we had met in the deep South. *Especially* from the North—where a psychological interpretation of distant street violence was understandably appealing. In the South, at the clinical conferences we occasionally attended, the categorical approximation made was a bit more social in nature: "the hoodlum element," or "poor white trash," or again, "a redneck community."

Tobacco Sharecropper, Southern Georgia, 1938

One day we spent a couple of hours with a white New Orleans fireman and his family, and I put each person through a few episodes of questioning, accepted politely and patiently by them. On the way home, I catalogued blind spots and worse. Suddenly, my wife brought me up short: "How many people in this world, including both of us, could survive the kind of scrutiny you give these people? You point out all these things about them. But what if you went into some home in Wellesley, Massachusetts, or Lincoln or Concord, Massachusetts, or yes, Cambridge, Massachusetts, near Harvard Square, and stayed there long enough, and were allowed to ask your questions? How many well-to-do people up there would even put up with it? And if you were given reasonably honest answers, not clever evasions, then wouldn't you come up with some similar evidence—people with their own, distinct ways of putting things, their own choices to make, and people who had their own kind of prejudices, narrowness, and even ignorance?"

Eventually all social investigators must confront these questions, if they are to perform their tasks with any level of competence, much less imagination and skill. Lange deftly solved the problem of intellectual predisposition and prejudice. She knew the literature of her subject matter—the government investigations, the political speeches, the regional histories, the economic and social surveys. Her habit was always to research after the fact, after the photographic expedition. She dismissed the practice lightly, saying her reading was simply "to see if my instincts were right." They were instincts of considerable sophistication. She spoke often of the need for blankness, the value of the receptive eye in photography. First came the image, then the research that interlocked the intricate features of the history she was recording. Obviously this is the closest anyone can approach to objectivity. Less obvious is the rarity of such practice, the passion for comprehensive understanding, particularly among photographers who often sacrifice breadth and profundity, in the name of visual purity.

Too much advance preparation affects more than the openness of the observer; it can have a decisive effect on the observed. Again, my most memorable lesson in this aspect of documentary reportage came from my own family, always ready to participate actively—and criticize vigorously. I preceded work among the Pueblo or Hopi Indians, among Chicanos or Alaska's Eskimos, in Appalachia or urban ghettos by reading all that I could get my hands on. I remember once, as we packed for a move to New Mexico, my wife's annoyance, her downright anger. Why all that tonnage of reading matter to go along? I can remember my three sons nodding and adding that besides, "we didn't have room for a big box of books," and besides, I would see "everything important," and besides "the Indians might discover that I had read all the books first and they would think I was cheating"—that last from an eight-year-old boy who has always been able to clothe the most devastating critique in what others will call a child's language.

I learned that both Indians and Eskimos have a sharp eye out for exactly the kind of mind, full of this or that self-important preconception, that my son, in his "child's" language, had given them credit for having. Repeatedly, in New Mexico and Arizona and Alaska, I found myself talking with Indians or Eskimos who would gradually grow more and more silent; then, aware of my compensatory talkativeness, let me in on their perceptions through a question or two—for instance: "Have you heard about us from people?" America's present-day problems are appreciated in the so-called backwaters as well as by Tokyo and London financiers. The "news" does filter—"down," "abroad the land," into the minds and hearts of a people. Welfare workers tell their clients of our troubles. Sheriffs remind already intimidated "minority groups" or the marginal and vulnerable by virtue of class, employment, education. Teachers let their pupils know what is happening. Bosses tell their workers. Indian chiefs get the word from Washington, as do Eskimos, who also are quite tied up with the federal government. And there is television, binding us more than we may realize—an endless ream of shared images and words.

The upshot is that the people we are supposed to be observing observe us, make decisions (often charitably and kindly) about letting us see what they think we want to see. No one ever put the case better to me than an Appalachian yeoman, a so-called mountaineer, who had just been visited by a documentary film crew.

They came here last year, with cameras. They were television people. They said they wanted to show the whole world how we live, and we thought it would help us out if they did. They said we should just go about being as we are, but they wouldn't let us be as we are. How could we—with them snapping their little cameras and running their big cameras, and asking us to go here and go there and try to look this way and look the other way? Finally, my oldest boy came to me and said he was tired of all of them, and he was going to leave and stay in the woods, up the hollow, until it was quiet here, and they were all gone.

They left, finally. They kept on trying to get us to say we're in bad shape. They kept on pointing out how we don't have this and we don't have that. They took pictures of us doing everything—well, almost *everything! But, I ask you, what will the people who see the pictures think? They'll think bad of us, I guess—sorry for us. They'll pity us. I'd like to talk with every one of them. I'd like*

Tuck's Filling Station, Route 501, Person County, North Carolina, 1939

to tell them we're in trouble, sure; we don't have the easiest life. But we're not the way they want to point us out to be. We're God-fearing people, and we have our pride in ourselves, and we're going to meet the Lord with our heads up high, and that's the most important thing in this life. . . .

The man who was the head of the television crew, and the newspaper man with him—on the day they left they asked me: what would you want, if you could wish it right now, and the wish would come true? Damned if I didn't draw a blank. The only thing that crossed my mind was something I couldn't say—that they'd leave, real fast. . . . When they were gone, finally, I took a big breath in, and I unbent myself. We all started smiling, and we had a good laugh. For a few minutes we looked around: they might still be there, picturing us one more time! But no, they truly were gone! My wife said to me: too bad they didn't get us this time, having some fun for ourselves! But if they'd been about, we wouldn't be the way we are with ourselves when we're alone.

A danger threatens all of us who leave one world, spend time in another one, then return to our original point of departure. None of us armed with cameras and tape recorders, no matter our conviction of empathy and sympathy, can be quite sure that we do not inadvertently fall into the pitfalls tactfully but knowingly suggested by that Appalachian.

Lange's way of avoiding those pitfalls was simply to efface herself. She abandoned credentials; she wasn't there to talk about herself, her motives. She was a casually dressed, alert woman who asked direct questions, then pulled out her cameras. She might, as she progressed, identify herself as a government photographer. Taylor's methods, the model of her own, succeeded by their nonthreatening casualness: he didn't interrogate—he talked with people, engaged in conversation, and the data he needed just "slipped out." How well it worked is suggested by the fact that only once, in all those years of travel and investigation, was he asked for identification—from those six justifiably suspicious Texas tenant farmers who had been deprived of jobs and the right to vote, and were ready to "whup" somebody.

An even greater problem for those who do documentary work exists on the ethical level: the very nature of the work risks injustice. But that does not mean the work is evil or should not be attempted. When the critic Susan Sontag in *On Photography* uses words such as "aggression," "imperial," and "capture"; and when she talks about photography as a "tool of power"; and when

Corner of Tobacco Farmer's Front Room, Person County, North Carolina, 1939

Outside FSA Grant Office, Calipatria, California, 1939

she declares that photographs enable people to take "possession" of the past, of space, of experience—she is echoing a Victorian scrupulosity which is, of course, inadequate. In whose name, in what name, are her moral misgivings and outright condemnations handed down? She worries about "consciousness and its acquisitive mood" and tells us the camera facilitates such a psychological process. No doubt cameras do indeed enable observers to grasp, to snap and then hold on tight, preserving moments from the lives of strangers as ornaments of the sighted bourgeoisie. But writers, too, can be charged with every sin Sontag calls upon in her sharp look at photographs and their various doings. Writers are full of the lusts she keeps referring to, the cannibalistic desire to absorb the world. Whether photographer, writer, or film maker, anyone who presumes to examine the lives of others must continually subject himself or herself to self-scrutiny, lest the pitfalls Sontag so narrowly ascribes to photography cloud the very goals he or she wishes to achieve.

A black minister in Greenwood, Mississippi, told my wife, one summer day in 1963, that he had been hearing more and more about "documentary" work:

I worry about who's doing the "documenting," and what a person has in mind to see—before they even get here to take a look at, take a listen! I say to myself: will they "document" our tears, but not our smiles? Will they "document" our rough times, but not show us having a good time, now and then—no matter how poor we be, and how down-and-out it gets for us, and how bad the treatment we receive from Mr. White Man? I know we need outsiders to lend us a hand. The people who run this county won't budge, unless they're pushed, and no one hereabouts who's got dark skin is going to push very long, without getting a bullet through the heart, or being pushed right into the Mississippi River!

But if people come here, and they want to help us, and they try to help us—but they end up thinking of us as only in trouble, and only in pain, and only persecuted—then we'll end up with the world getting the wrong picture about us. We'll end up appearing the way the Klan people want us to appear—as bad off as animals, and all the time whining, like a cat or a dog.

My wife and I have struggled with the issue of "balanced" reporting for many years, even as any number of documentary photographers have similarly weighed the scales: the practical political importance, for instance, of exposure, be it muckraking or under the auspices of social science; the countervailing matter of vulnerability exploited, pride wounded. I never had a chance to discuss that kind of equation with Dorothea Lange, but I did meet W. Eugene Smith, who spent his life photographing the needy from Haiti to Japan. He spoke eloquently on behalf of victims who need a voice, who need to be seen as witnesses to their suffering: "I believe the people I'm with know what I'm trying to do and want me to go ahead," he once told me. I wondered, however, whether there isn't some room for misunderstanding—for the observer to assume a

Gunlock County, Utah, 1953

commonality of analysis and purpose in his or her own interests.

My wife and I frequently used a Brownie camera in the course of our field studies and made a point of showing the pictures we took to the people we interviewed. We also played back for them the tapes of the statements they made to us. We were surprised, one afternoon, by a white yeoman woman who lived in northern Alabama, where the rural South is gently but significantly penetrated by the foothills of the Appalachian mountains. She put down a few "snaps," thought a few seconds, then offered her comments in a rapid-fire delivery:

I'm not sure I want to see myself. We've got no mirrors. We're not the kind who want to keep looking at ourselves. I don't believe the Bible wants you to be like that, all worried over appearances. In the store we go to, they have a mirror, and I look, I'll admit. We're all sinners! But to have a picture of myself, and it won't go away, it's just there, sitting and staring at you, and taking your mind away from other people, and your work, and fixing your thoughts on yourself—that's no good! My kids like to see themselves! But they're kids. I let them stare and stare at those snaps of yours. Then I sat them down and I said: "Children, you're staring at the devil!" They didn't know what I meant; so I explained.

Don't get me wrong, now! I'm not one of those hollering religious fanatics we have around here. I can take my religion, and I can leave it! But I believe there's a God, and His message is the right one—that we stop paying mind so much to ourselves! I see my kids grow up, and I see them getting "all puffed up," like the ministers say, like the Bible says. If you have a mirror ready, you'll look in it. If you have your picture nearby, you'll look at it. If you have a lot of time, and nothing to do, you'll sit and dream about yourself, and think about yourself. That's why I try to keep my kids on the go, all the time. I want them thinking of each other, not just themselves. I want us to be a self-supporting, self-respecting family. I don't want us wallowing in pity for ourselves, or being pitied by others, who've seen us on the television or seen pictures of us. I don't want us sitting here and staring at ourselves, and fixing ourselves up, so someone can take a good snap of us. Let them go snap elsewhere!

The ultimate, eternally worrisome question to be raised is this: to what extent does even the finest, most rigorous documentary effort serve the lie more than the truth? According to Susan Sontag, photographers are not only agents of covetousness, they also are doomed to a peculiar kind of extinction at the hands of "reality," which stubbornly defies the lens. A Hopi youth, a young woman of seventeen, once gave me a lecture on the camera that Sontag would have enjoyed, but only so much:

We don't need cameras here; we have enough trouble controlling our eyes! I waste my time looking and not seeing. If a camera helped us to see, we would be better off—but it would not be us, *seeing. A camera distracts you. It makes you less of a person. Words are even worse; they make birds fly away, and they make us dizzy with noise. Who can*

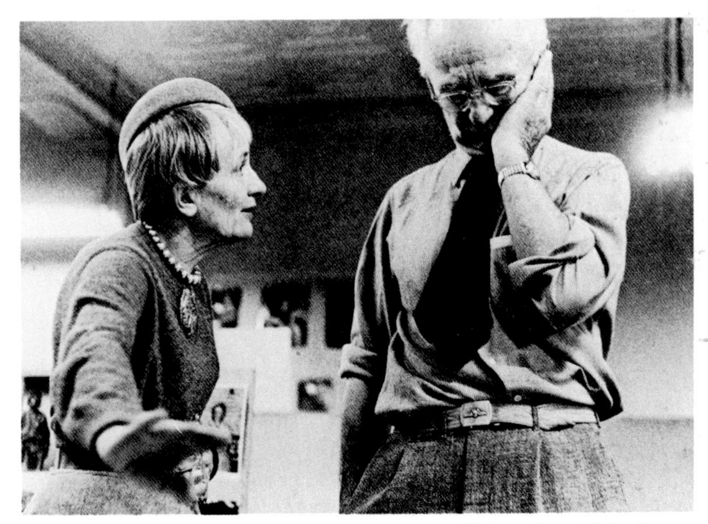

Dorothea Lange discussing preparation of "Family of Man" exhibit with Edward Steichen, c. 1954 (Wayne Miller)

At a photographic seminar, Aspen, Colorado, 1951 (Wayne Miller)

pay attention to the world, while someone chatters? The books of the Anglos are as noisy as their planes overhead. My mother says that the books fill up our head with words, and take over our eyes, too. We end up seeing what the words told us about. We stop seeing; *the noise of the words takes over. I have a cousin who is a New Hopi; he went to a BIA* [*Bureau of Indian Affairs*] *school, and lived with the Anglos in Albuquerque. He came back to us and he said that he doesn't look at the mesa anymore. He doesn't watch the clouds, see them meeting, leaving each other, doing a dance for us. He* thinks *about them; he* talks *to himself about them. He wishes his head could be quiet, the way it used to be. Stick with the Anglos, and you have a noisy head!*

Shown a photograph of a part of Arizona outside the Hopi reservation, that young woman smiled, looked immediately away toward the mesa, then came up with a surprising train of thought:

I've looked at the picture, and I want to go put it down on our mesa, and look at it, first, and then look at our mesa—back and forth. I'm afraid that if I just look at the picture, I'll forget what our own mesa looks like. My mother tells us to push the words away, keep them far away, when we look at the mesa. We stand; we look; we don't talk. When I talk with you about the mesa, I am taking its picture! Do you understand? I don't think you do! The Anglo teachers never understand. We see; they talk—and they want to take pictures, too!

I think that Lange had an intuitive grasp of the intrinsic distortion the young Hopi woman expressed to me. Lange seldom raised the issue of "art"; she cared for the "resonance," the emotional impulse of the print—but not its perfection. Toward the end of her life, she invariably, and accurately, referred to photography as a "medium." She meant that word in its exact sense—a means of conveying something. To our great disadvantage we of this generation have yielded to Marshall McLuhan's banality that "the medium is the message." Stryker, Lange, and the other FSA photographers had another purpose in mind. They were obsessed with the realities of their time: they confronted not a "subject," an "example," or a "respondant"—they confronted circumstances and situations; they confronted "fellow human beings." They moved in the realm not of the abstract, but of the concrete—like William Carlos Williams, saying what he had to say not through a discussion of ideas, but "in things." In so doing those photographers defied even their employer, the Farm Security Administration.

For the best of reasons, the FSA wanted Lange's help in educating a nation—teaching its citizen voters what was wrong, sorely wrong, with an economy, by showing them how much wretchedness had suddenly come upon an advanced industrial nation. Yet her American people, her American land, her barns and stores and road scenes attest to a vitality, a perseverance, a willfulness; one can even find "beauty" in all that injury and perplexity—strong, handsome faces, vigorous bodies, attractive buildings, a grace and grandeur to the countryside, even its ailing parts. An artist has asserted herself, it can be said—no matter a strong interest in polemical statement, in argumentative portrayal. In her later, international work the same tension persists: Lange as the pained observer, herself reasonably well off, yet terribly cognizant of, responsive to the difficult situation of so many others; yet, Lange as the visual observer, the person whose sensibilities are extremely broad, and whose representational faculties are awake, energetic, stubborn, and refined. In Ireland, in Nepal, in Egypt, in Korea she saw extreme poverty. She also saw objects to admire; scenes to record in all their striking charm or symmetry; faces of men, women, and children whose dignity, whose inviting loveliness simply could not be denied or overlooked.

Amana Society, Iowa, 1941

After the final, painful dismissal from the FSA Lange was very hurt, frustrated. She was in her mid-forties, at the height of her powers. To return to studio work was unthinkable—she was committed to the direction her photography had taken during the past seven years. She was hooked on the event, on history, and she knew she had the gift for photographing its most telling moments.

"History" was in turmoil all around her. In California war industries attracted hundreds of thousands of new, now successful job seekers. During the next ten years she would, either on assignment or driven solely by an inner need, aim her cameras at the changing land, the factories, the American people. Stryker's assumption that the major photo magazines would instantly pick her up was wrong. She was, with some justice, typed as a specialist on rural poverty. It was a subject that would indeed remain close to her heart, because it was ever close to Taylor's heart. But, for America's magazines, that phase of our history was ended, was no longer newsworthy. The spotlight was on war—the battles abroad and the mobilization on the home front.

In 1941 Lange, Taylor, and their children moved into a new home, the first they had owned. It was an open redwood-and-glass structure flooded with light, set on a tree- and plant-covered hill. Here, they would live for the rest of their lives. Here, she created an atmosphere of order and beauty, with simple, Shaker-like furniture, with bowls, pottery, and basketry from the regions where she had worked.

From time to time, she received assignments from a government agency, the Bureau of Agricultural Economics. In 1941, a Guggenheim Fellowship freed her for a project covering a different kind of settlement, the utopian communities. Taylor and Lange spent weeks among the Hutterites of South Dakota, the Amana Society in Iowa, and the Mormons in Utah. While they were away, all five children stayed with Taylor's first wife, an indication of an unusual civility in the separations and divorces that preceded their marriage. Lange never finished the Guggenheim project, however, because the war furnished her with another, perfectly suited to her convictions, to her feeling for the oppressed, and to her genius for chronicling the effects of dislocation.

Almost immediately after the declaration of war, the Roosevelt Administration issued the now infamous Executive Order 9066. Over 100,000 Japanese-Americans were suddenly rounded up, their homes, businesses, and farms virtually confiscated—sold at tremendous loss. Among them were Japanese-born Issei, and more than 70,000 Nisei, second-generation Americans and full citizens. The Army hastily erected camps, politely designated as Resettlement Centers. Lange and Taylor were stunned by the injustice, outraged as they watched among the victims some of his most brilliant students at the University of California.

Oddly enough, the Office of War Information wanted to document the internments, perhaps to show that the Nisei were being well treated, perhaps to demonstrate that the "enemy" had been domestically contained. No such camps, of course, were established for Americans of German or Italian descent, nor were the Japanese-Americans of Hawaii interned. Any American of Japanese descent on the West Coast lost freedom for the duration.

The OWI hired both Lange and Ansel Adams as official photographers. Her pictures, beautifully captioned as always, count among her major accomplishments as a photographer. Perhaps even more than the FSA photographs, they show her deep identification with, and compassion for the victim. Working for OWI, however, was a different experience. These were not pictures the government was anxious to release. She and Adams

Judge Fox, Oakland, California, 1957

were often accompanied by a military officer, and she in particular was at times treated virtually as a spy. One particular nemesis, an army major, enjoyed inspecting her equipment, impounding her film. Most of the Lange photographs of the Nisei lay in vaults until after the war.

In 1945, she was asked by the State Department to photograph the San Francisco conference that established the United Nations. She accepted, with misgivings. Her stomach was always delicate, a continuing hindrance even during the halycon thirties when she traveled tens of thousands of miles. The symptoms were becoming more severe. Ignoring her doctor's advice, she went ahead with the UN assignment. Shortly afterward, she was seized with violent pain and hospitalized. For the next eight years, severe ulcers kept her from attempting any camera work away from home, and on several occasions nearly killed her.

As a result, Lange did, finally, get to stay with her family in the redwood house. The longing had always been there, the guilt about allowing her children to be raised by friends and relatives had never ceased. The internal bleeding may have had at least some origin in the conflict between work and home. Now, and for the rest of her life, Lange would find her joy, her interests, and indeed some of her final best images in the family, the setting of the home, the simple objects in her kitchen and studio. Yet, there remained for her projects that would bring added fame and distant travels.

In the mid-1950s, her energy returning, Lange undertook a series of assignments for *Life* and *Look*. With Adams, she photographed a Mormon settlement in Utah; later, she accomplished two extraordinary photo essays, one on the public defender system in the California courts, the other, a haunting, beautiful vision of rural people in Ireland. At the close of the decade, through the beginning of the sixties, Taylor held various appointments as an international consultant on rural settlements and agrarian sociology. Lange feared her health would not stand up to wide-ranging travels in Latin America, Asia, the Middle East. But she found most sensible a doctor's opinion: "What difference does it make if you die over there or here? Go!" She went.

The experience was unlike any she had had before. She did not travel with Taylor as his working partner; she had no control over the nature of the projects or the itinerary. She was nearly stoned by mobs in Alexandria, Egypt; threatened by a hostile crowd in Korea; viewed in many places with suspicion or outright contempt. Nevertheless, one by one, the images emerged. Now she was weaker, her gift of establishing rap-

At Steep Ravine, Spring 1961

Pauly Taylor and Poulie, Steep Ravine, Spring 1961

port with people, of being an empathic participant in their lives impaired. Yet upon occasion her great power returned—a child's face in Korea, an upraised hand in a dance in Bali, a line of heavily veiled farm women in Egypt, and others. Once home she was delighted, proud that she had been around the world, had survived malaria and repeated bouts with ulcers.

In 1964, Lange at last completed *The American Country Woman,* a book that was a celebration of spirit, courage, good sense, and good humor. It was then that she learned that the newest of her abdominal pains would not be cured. The doctors diagnosed terminal cancer. Lange and Taylor accepted the decision with what can only be called grace.

Her final project, the one that now meant the most to her, was "To a Cabin," a photographic study of her children and their children at the beach cottage at Steep Ravine. She turned from that study, reluctantly abandoned it, when The Museum of Modern Art's curator of photography, John Szarkowski, informed her—didn't ask; he knew she would resist—that he planned a major retrospective exhibition of her work. Only a half dozen photographers had ever been so honored.

The final two years of Lange's life were devoted to a review of her lifetime's work. From tens of thousands of negatives she and Szarkowski selected the 200 prints to be exhibited; painstakingly they arranged, balanced, and harmonized the images, panel by panel. Curator and photographer worked well together; they knew when to admire one another and when to argue. She would plead for pictures that told a story she liked; he would suggest the picture that had the greatest impact as an image—the superior picture.

She worked and worked hard—at times exhausted after only twenty minutes of effort. She was afraid—not of the illness, not of death. She was confronting a lifetime of work, and worried about its worth. But, as she told an interviewer making a film of her, "When you get to the point I'm at, there's no point to anything *but* risks."

And there was one other issue about which she cared passionately. There would be no more photographs by Dorothea Lange. But who would be recording the still rapidly changing face of America, a nation whose citizens had embarked on a path of unprecedented urbanization? In the city, far more than the country, the new social patterns were taking shape. To everyone who came within earshot, she spoke of the need for a project, modeled along the lines of the FSA, to capture this part of our history. On the very day she died, October 11, 1965, Dorothea Lange was still the documentary field worker—trying to wrest the truth for others to see. Her retrospective exhibition opened three months after her death.

Dyanna Taylor, Steep Ravine, Spring 1961

Dyanna Taylor at Steep Ravine, Spring 1961

Dorothea Lange's studio, Berkeley, c. 1964 (Helen Dixon)

Dorothea Lange and Richard Conrat laying out prints for her Museum of Modern Art exhibition, 1965 (Rondal Partridge)

Dorothea Lange's studio, Berkeley, c. 1964 (Helen Dixon)

Dorothea Lange and John Szarkowski reviewing prints for her show at The Museum of Modern Art, 1965 (Shirley C. Burden)

There is a road—narrow, pitted, foreboding—that cuts straight through empty Texas flatlands. It is a road that offers no prospect, no hope—except for more of the same, endlessly. On the day in 1938 when Dorothea Lange photographed the road, and called it *Migrant Route*, there was not a soul upon it (a rare picture for Lange, one without people), yet it is packed with presences, crowded, we sense, with hundreds upon hundreds of thousands of men, women, and children. From somewhere, these farmers and their families had been driven to take this road, and others like it, by financial collapse; by machines that made their labor valueless; by Nature herself, gathering up the soil and hurling it off the land in unimaginable airborne tidal waves of dust. We know who these people were who drove, pushed handcarts, hitchhiked, walked those roads. We know because she made us look at them, look into their faces.

She photographed them on that, and many other roads, and she followed them back to their origins, back to where the trouble started. And she followed them to their destination. An enormous voyage of discovery and rediscovery, to nameless places, to villages almost too small to bear a name. Who was this photographer who visited, in 1936, such remote towns of Mississippi, as Hill House and Piney Woods and Kiln; who visited that same year Eden, Alabama; and Blythville, Arkansas; and Tombstone, Arizona; and Odessa, Texas; and Ostee Cachr, Oklahoma; and Social Circle, Georgia? All those places and more! Why did she do it, plunge through Georgia, her own kind of Sherman, not content with Atlanta, not content, even, with Waycross and Valdosta and Americus, reasonably well-known towns and agricultural centers? *Social Circle, Georgia!* A village of about a thousand in the 1930s, a village that belongs to Walton County, east of Atlanta; a village not far from *Between*, near *Gratis*; a village, finally, whose sleepy distance from San Francisco or New York seemed infinite then and still does.

Certainly, Dorothea Lange's extended itinerary during those summers of the 1930s, when her artistic and social interests burst into a harmonious flowering, was a tribute to her will and strength of heart. She brought to Social Circle, after all, her own circles. Circles of illness and pain: a leg she had to drag—the residue of that early polio; and a stomach that never was very good at digesting food; and a nervous, irritable temperament that taxed her, wearied her even as it drove her on. Circles of human involvement: two young sons of her own, and with the marriage to Paul Taylor, stepchildren—all left behind, as their mother took pictures of other mothers, struggling to make do with other children. One hears, from her own lips, in documentaries made of her, about the struggle she waged as an artist who kept on the move so steadily, leaving behind a family—children who must have missed her so very much for just the reasons others posed for her, or let her hover nearby: this was an engaging woman, tenacious of spirit and immensely responsive to others. She must have been sorely missed in California, while she passed through Social Circle, Georgia.

Her obvious affiliation with the Romantic tradition must have been encouraged by the inner turmoil she could not have helped feeling. The Romantics have always fed off their own anguish. She had to struggle against not just Southern imperatives, but the general psychological standards of a particular time. She had to struggle with her conscience, her sense of what ought to be—not only for the Okies or the 'croppers or the hillbillies; but for the children of Dorothea Lange and Maynard Dixon, the children of her beloved Paul Taylor, left time and again for the joint pursuits carried on by a photographer and a social economist whose other "children" were, of course, the thousands and thousands of readers and viewers of, say, *An American Exodus*. She re-

Lange-Taylor family, Berkeley, 1965 (Pirkle Jones)

turned, of course, to her family. She clung to it with great ardor, maybe more of it than suited its members upon occasion. One hears that her sons waited for her death before getting divorced, so adamant was she upon an intactness to their life, her life—an intactness whose value she appreciated keenly, let us say, out of the depths of her complex and sometimes deeply pained existence. A filmed interview, made shortly before her death, shows the old dilemma—the old torture once more visiting the victim, who had become receptive to a certain fate: whether to spend her last energies helping to bring about a Dorothea Lange retrospective show, or to spend those precious, irreplaceable moments with her family.

Such torment was, of course, not hers alone. Millions of women, and, in their own fashion, men, have to struggle with the contrary demands of their home life, their working life. It would be absurd if we were to dwell on the vicissitudes of Lange's family life, even those occasioned by her sex, in any psychologically reductive way: *this* explains or prompted *that*. There was talent, and, for her, that talent had to be realized. To be sure, behind her achievements were the usual accidents, incidents, moments of chance and luck that helped along that achievement. A person met. A lesson learned. Even a historic moment—the seeming collapse of an entire nation, and what such a development meant to Walker Evans and James Agee, to Ben Shahn and Dorothea Lange. Without question, there is a driven side to many talented people who end up becoming well-known, successful—a side whose various elements can be surmised, teased out, set down, placed in some causal connection, each to the other.

The evidence is at hand: her visions. Children being held. Children near at hand, and if feckless in their lot (the poor, the rural down-and-out, the minorities), then fortunate in their immediate situations as boys or girls whose mothers or fathers, often enough, seem (for all the vulnerability of their lives) physically strong, spiritually honorable. People at work—menial work, commonly, even back-breaking work, but work done, not shunned. People on a search: a new home, a job, some food—active and pressing; sometimes entrepreneurial, sometimes eagerly scrutinizing. And those hands, detached and strong, detached and ever so open and subject to injury; or hard on the job, pulling and pushing, clasping and grabbing, holding and letting go.

One feels, too, her continuing love affair with the American land, and later, the soil of Europe, the Middle East, Asia. Even the Dust Bowl of the middle 1930s comes off as a powerful giant, wounded, but by no means fatally so. Just as

Dorothea Lange in her kitchen, Berkeley, 1964 (Rondal Partridge)

Dining Room Table, Berkeley, 1964 (Rondal Partridge)

Steinbeck's characters in *The Grapes of Wrath* seemed too wise and too good for us to despair completely when contemplating their fate, Lange's displaced farmers or underpaid and vulnerable fieldhands win our confidence in not only their virtue but their future. No country whose government, after all, has subsidized such tender and affectionate glimpses; no country whose rural "*lumpenproletariat*" seems so sturdy and appealing (white) or so bravely, wisely enduring (black) is in danger of the violent deterioration of social and political structures this century at one point (the 1930s) seemed determined to visit upon the entire industrial West.

It is fitting in connection with Lange's work to reflect on William Carlos Williams and Walt Whitman, even on those decidedly aristocratic, wonderfully astute observers of America, Alexis de Tocqueville and Henry James. The last of these may have summarized it all—what any of us who try to do "documentary studies" can only hope to do with a small quota of his brilliantly penetrating success: "The manners, the manners," his terse mandate of what must be seen, what must be set down for others to see. Whitman was more celebratory, less dispassionate. Williams was a fiery enthusiast, a mordant critic, if not vigorous combatant. The French visitor de Tocqueville was less literary than James, more systematic in his elegant, nineteenth-century prophesy not only of America's coming history, but a new division of intellectual activity—the so-called social sciences. Lange reveals elements of all those observers in her work. In the Jamesian tradition, she can concentrate on the distinctive appearance of a woman's neck, on the complementary splendor of two shoes, on the extended power of a particular barn's sloping roof. She can roam America, follow its various roads, large and small, marvel at the variety and robustness of our people—in the tradition of Whitman: a gentle and loving, but also a tough, willful, and resourceful traveler, determined to return home with productive, inspiring memories. She can shake her fists—as Williams used to do—at the stupidity of so many, the needless injuries to people who deserve better; and like him, she can summon a redemptive, celebratory music in response to what she has seen others experience, and through them, herself experienced. She can even be the careful analytic student de Tocqueville was—those hands she gives us, those tools, those clothes, those signs; in sum, those physical aspects of existence that reveal so much about a given people's aspirations and difficulties.

Dorothea Lange was finally another restless visionary artist, using film to make the point novelists and poets and painters and photographers and sculptors all keep trying to make: I am here; I hear and see; I will take what my senses offer my brain and with all my might offer others something they can see or hear, and doing so, be informed, be startled, be moved to awe and wonder, be entertained, be rescued from the banality, the dreary silliness this world, inevitably, presses upon us. She failed at times; failed personally, as she herself acknowledged, when she discussed the many leaves of absence from her home, her young children; failed artistically, when she lapsed into the photographer's version of coyness, rhetorical overstatement, repetitive posturing. But she succeeded repeatedly—gave us our rock-bottom selves: a clear and trenchant portrait of any number of this earth's twentieth-century people.

Dorothea at home, Berkeley, 1964
(Richard Conrat)

Life for people begins to crumble on the edges;
they don't realize it. But this particular section was
not far from the place where my studio was,
and I observed some things that were happening.
My powers of observation are fairly good, and I have used them;
I like to use them. Sometimes I'm aware of what's going on
behind me, you know. My angle of vision was almost
360 degrees. That's training. But I have done
some photographs of this. One of them is my most famed
photograph. I made that on the first day
I ever went in an area where people said, "Oh, don't go there."
It was on the first day that I ever made a
photograph actually on the street.

White Angel Bread Line, San Francisco, 1932

For me documentary photography is less a matter of
subject *and more a matter of* approach. *The important*
thing is not what's *photographed but* how. . . .
My own approach is based upon three considerations.
First—hands off! Whatever I photograph,
I do not molest or tamper with or arrange.
Second—a sense of place. Whatever I photograph, I try
to picture as part of its surroundings, as having roots.
Third—a sense of time. Whatever I photograph, I try
to show as having its position in the past
or in the present. But beyond these three things,
the only thing I keep in mind is that—well
there it is, that quotation pinned on my darkroom door:

"The contemplation of things as they are,
without substitution or imposture,
without error or confusion,
is in itself a nobler thing
than a whole harvest of invention."
—Francis Bacon

The General Strike, San Francisco, 1934

Demonstration, San Francisco, 1934

Demonstration, San Francisco, 1934

Man Beside Wheelbarrow, San Francisco, 1934

I'd begun to get a much firmer grip on the things I really wanted to do in my work. This photograph of the man with his head on his arms for instance—five years earlier, I would have thought it enough to take a picture of a man, no more. But now, I wanted to take a picture of a man as he stood in his world—in this case, a man with his head down, with his back against the wall, with his livelihood, like the wheelbarrow, overturned.

Unemployed Men on Howard Street, San Francisco, 1937

I said, "I will set myself a big problem. I will go down there, I will photograph this thing, I will come back, and develop it. I will print it and I will mount it and I will put it on the wall, all in 24 hours. I will do this to see if I can grab a hunk of lightning."

May Day Listener, San Francisco, 1934

Salvation Army, San Francisco, 1939

Funeral Cortege, End of an Era in a Small Valley Town, California, 1938

It's a very difficult thing to be exposed to the new
and strange worlds that you know nothing about
and find your way. That's a big job.
It's hard, without relying on past performances and
finding your own little rut, which comforts you.
It's a hard thing to be lost.

Hop Harvesting, Wheatland, California, 1935

Hop Harvesting, Wheatland, California, 1935

Hop Harvesting, Wheatland, California, 1935

Family on the Road, Midwest, c. 1938

They looked very woebegone to me. . . . I looked at the license plate on the car and it was Oklahoma. I got out and asked which way were they going . . . And they said, "We've been blown out. . . ." They were the first arrivals that I saw. These were the people who got up that day quick and left. They saw they had no crop back there. They had to get out. All of that day . . . I saw these people; and I couldn't wait—I photographed them.

Three Generations of Texans, 1935

Oklahoma Drought Refugees, 1935

Their roots were all torn out. The only background they had was a background of utter poverty. It's very hard to photograph a proud man against a background like that, because it doesn't show what he's proud about. I had to get my camera to register the things about those people that were more important than how poor they were—their pride, their strength, their spirit.

Ditched, Stalled, and Stranded, San Joaquin Valley, California, 1935

Housing for Migrant Workers, Coachella Valley, California, 1935

Dairy Co-op Officials, 1935

Back, 1938

Back, 1935

You know, so often it's just sticking around and being there, remaining there, not swooping in and swooping out in a cloud of dust; sitting down on the ground with people, letting children look at your camera with their dirty, grimy little hands, and putting their fingers on the lens, and you let them, because you know that if you will behave in a generous manner, you're very apt to receive it, you know? Those kinds of things. I don't mean to say I did that all the time, but I remember that I have done it, and I have asked for a drink of water and taken a long time to drink it, and I have told everything about myself long before I asked the question "What are you doing here?"

They'd say, "With your camera? What do you want to take pictures of us for? Why don't you go down and do this, that, and the other?" I've taken a long time, patiently, to explain, and as truthfully as I could.

Jobless on Edge of Pea Field, Imperial Valley, California, 1937

Carrot Fieldworkers, probably the San Joaquin Valley, c. 1935

Filipinos Cutting Lettuce, Salinas, California, 1935

Hoe Cutter, near Anniston, Alabama, 1936

I can only say I knew I was looking at something.
You know there are moments such as these when time
stands still and all you do is hold your breath
and hope it will wait for you. And you
just hope you will have time enough to get it organized
in a fraction of a second on that tiny piece
of sensitive film. Sometimes you have an inner sense
that you have encompassed the thing generally.
You know then that you are not taking anything away from
anyone: their privacy, their dignity, their wholeness.

Drought Refugees from Oklahoma, Blythe, California, 1936

Texas Panhandle, 1938

The Sheriff of McAlester, Oklahoma, in Front of the Jail, 1936

It was raining, the camera bags were packed, and I had on the seat
beside me in the car the results of my long trip,
the box containing all those rolls and packs of exposed film
ready to mail back to Washington. It was a time of relief.
Sixty-five miles an hour for seven hours would get me home to my family
that night, and my eyes were glued to the wet and gleaming highway
that stretched out ahead. I felt freed,
for I could lift my mind off my job and think of home.

I was on my way and barely saw a crude sign with pointing arrow
which flashed by at the side of the road, saying PEA-PICKERS CAMP.
But out of the corner of my eye, I did *see it. . . .*

Having well convinced myself for 20 miles that I could continue on,
I did the opposite. Almost without realizing what I was doing,
I made a U-turn on the empty highway. I went back those
20 miles and turned off the highway at that sign, PEA-PICKERS CAMP.

I was following instinct, not reason; I drove
into that wet soggy camp and parked my car like a homing pigeon.

I saw and approached the hungry and desperate mother,
as if drawn by a magnet. I do not remember how I explained my
presence or my camera to her, but I do remember she asked me
no questions. . . . She told me her age, that she was 32.
She said that they had been living on frozen vegetables
from the surrounding fields, and birds that the children killed.
She had just sold the tires from her car to buy food.
There she sat in that lean-to tent with her children huddled
around her, and seemed to know that my pictures might help her,
and so she helped me. There was a sort of equality about it.

Migrant Mother, Nipomo, California, 1936

FSA Rehabilitation Clients. Near Wapato, Yakima Valley, Washington, 1939

Alabama Farm, c. 1938

Woman of the High Plains, Texas Panhandle, 1938

Woman of the high plains: "If you die, you're dead—that's all."

Damaged Child, Shacktown, Elm Grove, Oklahoma, 1936

Drought farmers, Sallisaw, Sequoyah County, Oklahoma, 1936

Tractored Out, Childress County, Texas, 1938

Earlier, I'd gotten at people through the ways
they'd been torn loose, but now I had to get at them
through the ways they were bound up.
This photograph of the plantation overseer with his foot
on the bumper of his car is an example of what I mean,
and this one, too (of hands holding a primitive hoe).
In the first, I tried to photograph a man as he was
tied up with his fellow, and in the second,
a man as he was tied up with the land.

Plantation Overseer and His Field Hands, near Clarksdale, Mississippi, 1936.

Alabama farm, c. 1938

Crossroads Store, Alabama, 1937

Turpentine Dippers, Georgia, 1937

By the Chinaberry Tree, near Tipton, Georgia, 1938

Waterboy, Mississippi Delta, 1938

Greenville, Mississippi, 1938

Near Eutaw, Alabama, 1936

Ex-Slave with a Long Memory, Alabama, 1937

Ex-Slave with a Long Memory, Alabama, 1937

Accidentally learned at Gordonton that "everybody in the community was gathering at the church, going to take their dinner." Was not able to get back in time to see the dinner in progress and most of the cleaning done. Farm women of all ages, men and children; one six-month-old baby and one woman on two crutches were still there finishing up the cleaning at about 2:30. . . . Had to talk to a succession of people . . . had to ask the older members: had to talk to the head deacon to get permission to photograph. They very much want to have a print showing the church and the grounds. Very proud of their church, spacious well-shaded churchyard, well-kept (though very simple) cemetery. . . . The church is primitive Baptist . . . and is "over a hundred years old". . . . It has 70 members and "lots of friends around who help out." Preaching once a month and the church is crowded. Will probably hold 500. Cleaning the church consisted of sweeping, dusting, washing the windows; "we think we ought to keep it as nice as we do our homes. . . ." No picture taken inside the church because of hesitation of church members. The people were substantial, well-fed looking, the women in clean prints mostly ready-made, the men in clean shirts and trousers, some overalls. Good-looking children. Many addressed each other as cousin or aunt, etc. . . . A group of solid country people who live generously and well.

Group on church steps: note rakes, yard brooms made of dogwood, homemade buckets with dippers. Note woman wearing bonnet, front and side view. Note homemade gloves. This woman was named "Queen."

July 9 is "preachin' Sunday" and got permission from deacon to return to make pictures of the congregation.

Family Farmstead, Nebraska, 1940

Rural Rehabilitation Client, Tulare County, California, 1938

Church on the Great Plains, South Dakota, c. 1938

Gunlock County, Utah, 1953

South Dakota, 1939

One-Room School, Baker County, Oregon, 1939

Ma Burnham, Conway, Arkansas, 1938

Ma Burnham from Conroy, Arkansas: "My father was a Confederate soldier. He give his age a year older than what it was to get into the Army. After the war, he bought 280 acres from the railroad and cleared it. We never had a mortgage on it. They all owned their farms. . . .
We made all we ate and wore. We had a loom and wheel.
The old settlers had the cream. In '19 and '20 the land was sold and the money divided. Now none of the children own their land.
It's all done gone, but it raised a family. I've done my duty—I feel like I have. I've raised 12 children—6 dead, 6 alive, and 2 orphans."

Hands, Maynard and Dan Dixon, c. 1930

Woman of the High Plains, Texas Panhandle, 1938

These are women of the American soil. They are a hardy stock.
They are of the roots of our country. . . .They are not
our well-advertised women of beauty and fashion. . . .
These women represent a different mode of life. They are of
themselves *a very great American style. They live*
with courage and purpose, a part of our tradition.

Early Californian. Her family migrated after the Civil War from Deer Creek Plantation, Mississippi, to the great empty central valley of California, where she was born eighty-one years ago. The family traced lineage back to Williamsburg, Virginia—the first seventeenth-century settlement in America—and had been slaveholders. Now, she tends her flower garden on a Marin County hillside.

Rebecca Dixon, Sausalito, California, 1954

Abandoned Farm, near Dalhart, Texas, 1938

Grain Elevator, Everett, Texas, 1938

A documentary photograph is not a factual photograph per se.
[The documentary photograph] carries with it another thing,
a quality [in the subject] that the artist responds to.
It is a photograph which carries the
full meaning of the episode or the circumstance or
the situation that can only be revealed—because you
can't really recapture it—by this other quality. There
is no real warfare between the artist and the documentary
photographer. He has to be both. . . .
The documentary photographer is trying
to speak to you in terms of everyone's experience.

Homeless Family, Oklahoma, 1938

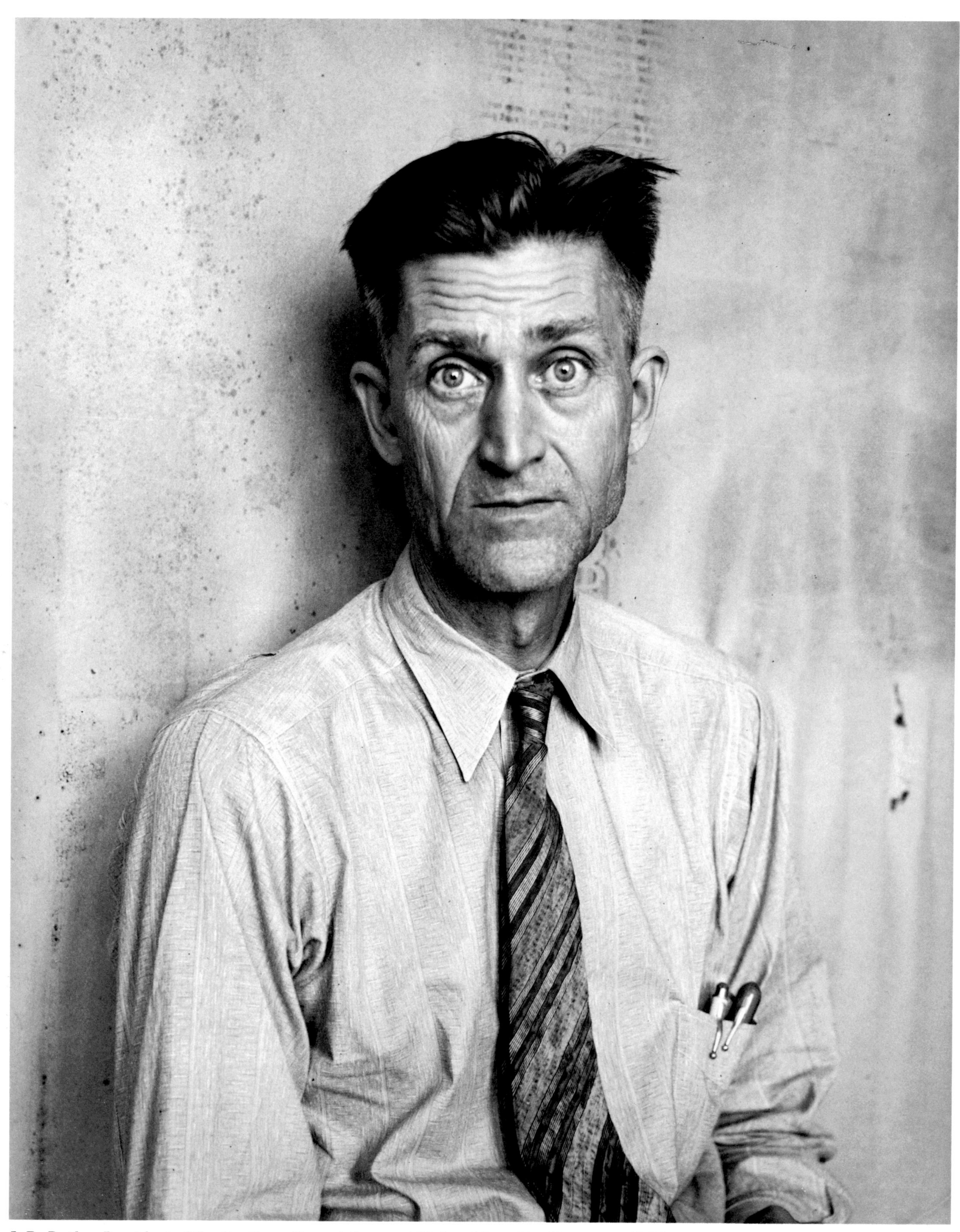

J. R. Butler, President of the Southern Tenant Farmers' Union, Memphis, Tennessee, 1938

Grayson, San Joaquin Valley, California, 1938

Mexican Migrant Fieldworker, Imperial Valley, California, 1937

The Road West, New Mexico, 1938

Ball Game, Migrant Camp, Shafter, California, 1938

Sometimes you stick around because hostility itself is important.
The people who are garrulous and wear their heart on their sleeve
and tell you everything, that's one kind of person;
but the fellow who's hiding behind a tree, and hoping you
don't see him, is the fellow you'd better find out about.

Kern County, California, 1938

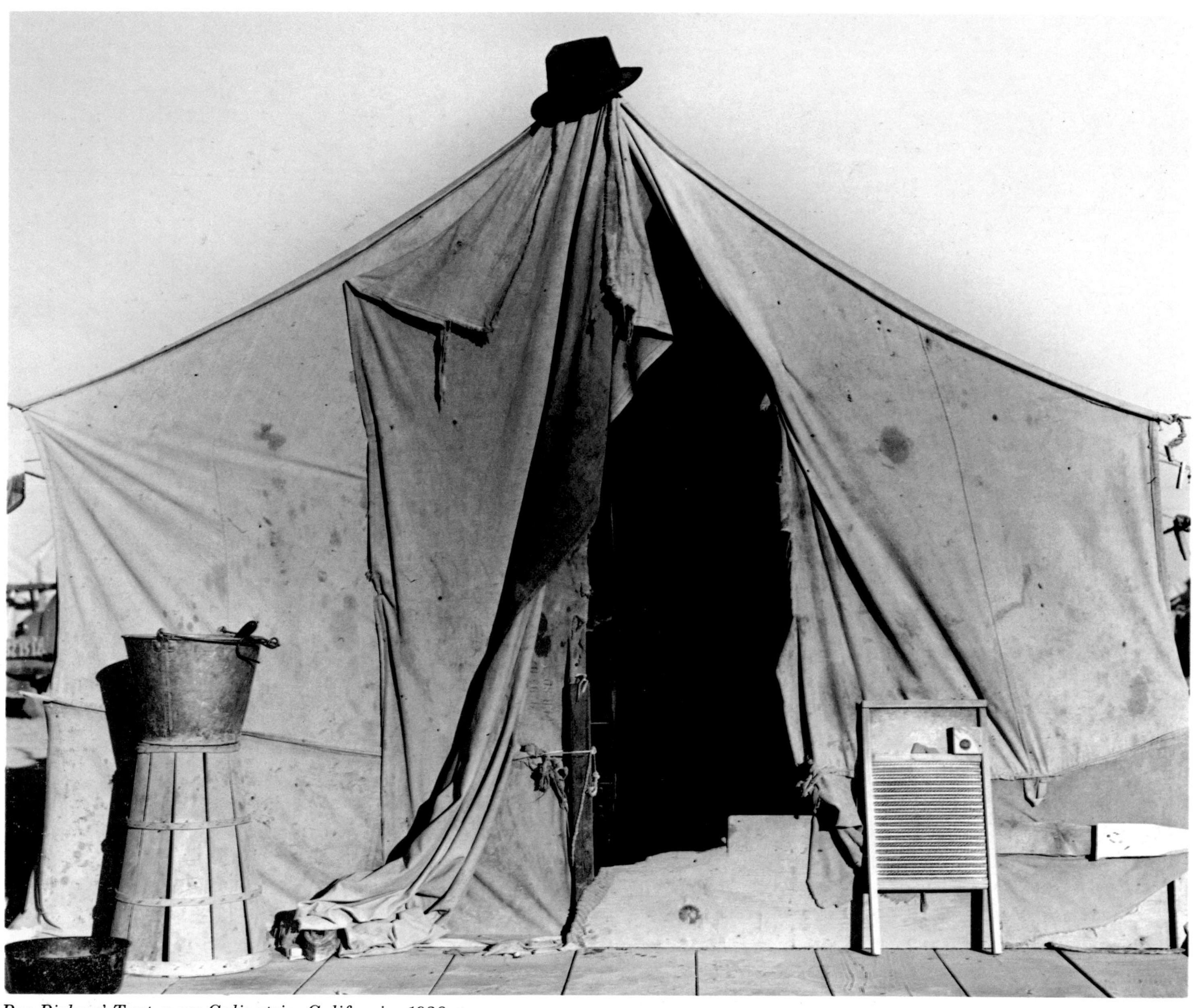

Pea-Pickers' Tent, near Calipatria, California, 1938

I had begun to talk to the people I photographed.
For some reason, I don't know why, the people in the city
were silent people, and we never spoke to each other.
But in the migrant camps, there were always talkers.
This was very helpful to me, and I think it was helpful to them.
It gave us a chance to meet on common ground—something a
photographer like myself must find if he's going to do good work.

Mother and Children, on the Road, Tulelake, Siskiyou County, California, 1939

Jake Jones's Hands, Gunlock County, Utah, 1953

Riverbank Gas Station, c. 1940

Tenant Farmers without Farms, Hardman County, Texas, 1937

I have a wife and one child, and I've been staying even on $22.80 a month by living close. I was $90 in debt when I started on WPA, and I'm still $90 in debt.

We used to go to church when we had better clothes. These are our Sunday clothes. All of us and our families together haven't spent $40 on clothes in the past year.

I'd be happy with a job at $1.50 a day.

Tenant Farmers without Farms, Hardman County, Texas, 1937

None of us vote. It costs us $3.50 poll tax
for a married man and wife to vote in Texas.

If we fight, who we gonna whup?

Give us something to do, and pay us a living wage.

We were born at the wrong time.
We ought to have died when we was young.

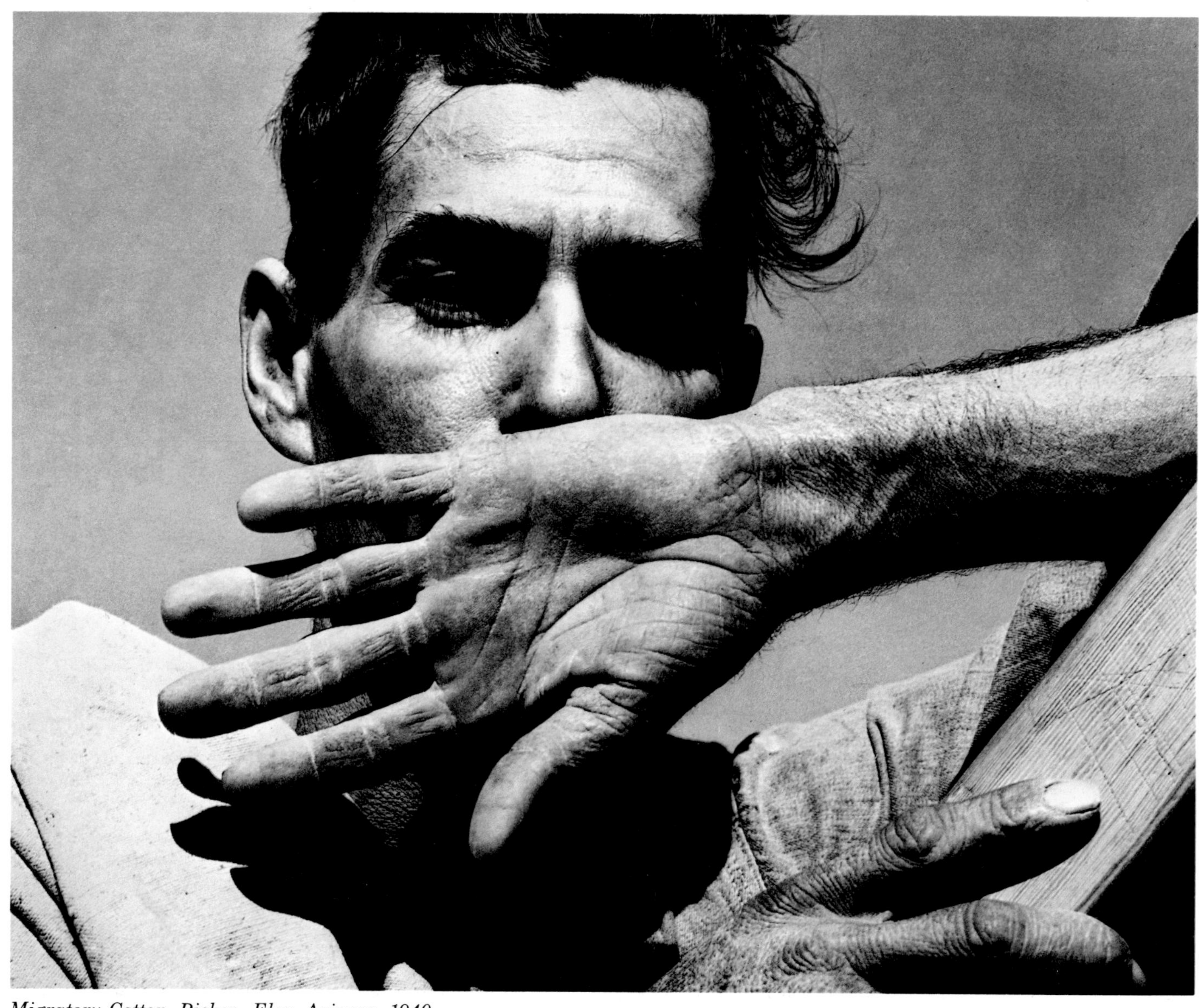

Migratory Cotton Picker, Eloy, Arizona, 1940

On the Great Plains, near Winner, South Dakota, 1938

Documentary photography records the social scene of our time. It mirrors the present and documents for the future. Its focus is man in his relation to mankind. It records his customs at work, at war, at play, or his round of activities through twenty-four hours of the day, the cycle of the seasons, or the span of a life. It portrays his institutions–family, church, government, political organizations, social clubs, labor unions. It shows not merely their façades, but seeks to reveal the manner in which they function, absorb the life, hold the loyalty, and influence the behavior of human beings. It is concerned with methods of work and the dependence of workmen on each other and on their employers. It is pre-eminently suited to build a record of change. Advancing technology raises standards of living, creates unemployment, changes the face of cities and of the agricultural landscape. The evidence of these trends—the simultaneous existence of past, present, and portent of the future—is conspicuous in old and new forms, old and new customs, on every hand. Documentary photography stands on its own merits and has validity by itself. A single photographic print may be "news," a "portrait," "art," or "documentary"—any of these, all of them, or none. Among the tools of social science—graphs, statistics, maps, and text—documentation by photograph now is assuming place. Documentary photography invites and needs participation by amateurs as well as by professionals. Only through the interested work of amateurs who choose themes and follow them can documentation by the camera of our age and our complex society be intimate, pervasive, and adequate.

San Francisco, California, 1939

Shipyard Construction Workers, Richmond, California, 1942

Shipyard Worker, Richmond, California, 1942

Everything is propaganda for what you believe in actually.
I don't see that it could be otherwise.
The harder and the more deeply you believe in anything,
the more in a sense you're a propagandist.
Conviction, propaganda, faith. I don't know, I never have
been able to come to the conclusion that that's a bad word.

End of Shift, Richmond, California, 1942

Argument in Trailer Court, 1944

New York City, 1952

Walking Wounded, Oakland, California, 1954

Well, I many times encountered courage, real courage.
Undeniable courage. I've heard it said that that
was the highest quality of the human animal. There is no other. . . .
Well, I encountered that many times, in unexpected places.
And I have learned to recognize it when I see it. Through that,
I dealt with people in a very sharp extreme.
I am not sure that quality is not dissipating in us as a people.

What I photographed was the procedure, the process of processing.
I photographed the normal life insofar as I could. . . . I photographed
. . . the Japanese quarter of San Francisco,
the businesses they were operating, and the people as they were
going to their YWCAs and YMCAs and churches
and in their Nisei headquarters, all the baffled,
bewildered people, whose own *people took it on themselves to*
describe it to them, to explain it to them. When the business of
their having shots and innoculations came, again
their own *people took it over. They refused army doctors.*
Their own doctors did it. Everything that was possible
that they could do themselves, they did—asked the minimum,
took huge sacrifices, made practically no demands . . .
and this I photographed, the long lines on the streets waiting,
for instance, as though they were going to an important event.
New clothes. . . . I photographed them on the buses,
on the trains, and I photographed their arrival in the assembly
centers. . . . It seems long ago and now . . . I was in the
Buddhist church the other day and I found myself for the
first time since those years, excepting when I was in Tokyo,
in my own country surrounded by these little black heads
in rows and rows. But it brought it all back to me.

Pledge of Allegiance at Rafael Weill Elementary School a Few Weeks Prior to Evacuation, San Francisco, 1942

Toquerville, Utah, 1953

Gothic Doorway, Toquerville, Utah, 1953

Café near Pinhole, California, 1956

U.S. Highway 40, California, 1956

Woman of the Far West welcomes friends gathering on Memorial Day in the old cemetery. This is an annual occasion and great day for the country people. They bring their lunches and stay all day in the valley, "visiting" with old associates and "cleaning up" the family graves.

Woman from Berryessa Valley, California, Memorial Day, 1956

Toquerville, Utah, 1953

Toquerville is a town with no bank,
no movie house, no garage, no motel,
no café. There is a post office and
two small grocery stores.
There is no neon sign.

Berryessa Valley, California, 1956

On the floor of an upper hall these relics–signs of severed roots–lay exactly like this. The home was completely empty, save for these abandoned portraits, a few old school books–and in the attic, some wooden curtain poles with round brass knobs at the ends.

All photographs—not only those that are so-called "documentary," and every photograph really is documentary and belongs in some place, has a place in history—can be fortified by words. I don't mean that they should have poetic captions. Any photographer looking out at the world he lives in does many things that will be valuable, even the commercial boys down on Shattuck Avenue, the fellows who do the wedding and school pictures. That's all documentary material of greatest interest, in so many ways. . . . I don't like the kind of written material that tells a person what to look for, or that explains the photograph. I like the kind of material that gives more background, that fortifies it without directing the person's mind. It just gives him more with which to look at the picture.

Country Road, County Clare, Ireland, 1954

Irish Child, County Clare, Ireland, 1954

Ireland, 1954

Boy in Landscape, Ireland, 1954

Ireland, 1954

Black Maria, Oakland, c. 1955–57

I find that it has become instinctive, habitual, necessary, to group photographs. I used to think in terms of single photographs, the bull's-eye technique. No more.

A photographic statement is more what I now reach for. Therefore these pairs, like a sentence of 2 words.

Here we can express the relationships, equivalents, progressions, contradictions, positives and negatives, etc., etc. Our medium is peculiarly geared to this.

Public Defender in Court, Oakland, California, 1957

The Defendant, Alameda County Courthouse, California, c. 1955–57

Public Defender, Alameda County Courthouse, California, c. 1955–57

To know ahead of time what you're looking for means
you're then only photographing your own preconceptions,
which is very limiting, and often false. . . .
I certainly wouldn't criticize a photographer who
works completely without plan, and photographs that
to which he instinctively responds. In fact,
a very good way to work is to open yourself as wide as
you can, which in itself is a difficult thing to do—
just to be like a piece of unexposed, sensitized material. . . .

Andrew, Berkeley, 1959

John and Helen, Berkeley, 1952

First Born, Berkeley, 1952

Winter, California, 1955

Bad Trouble over the Weekend, 1964

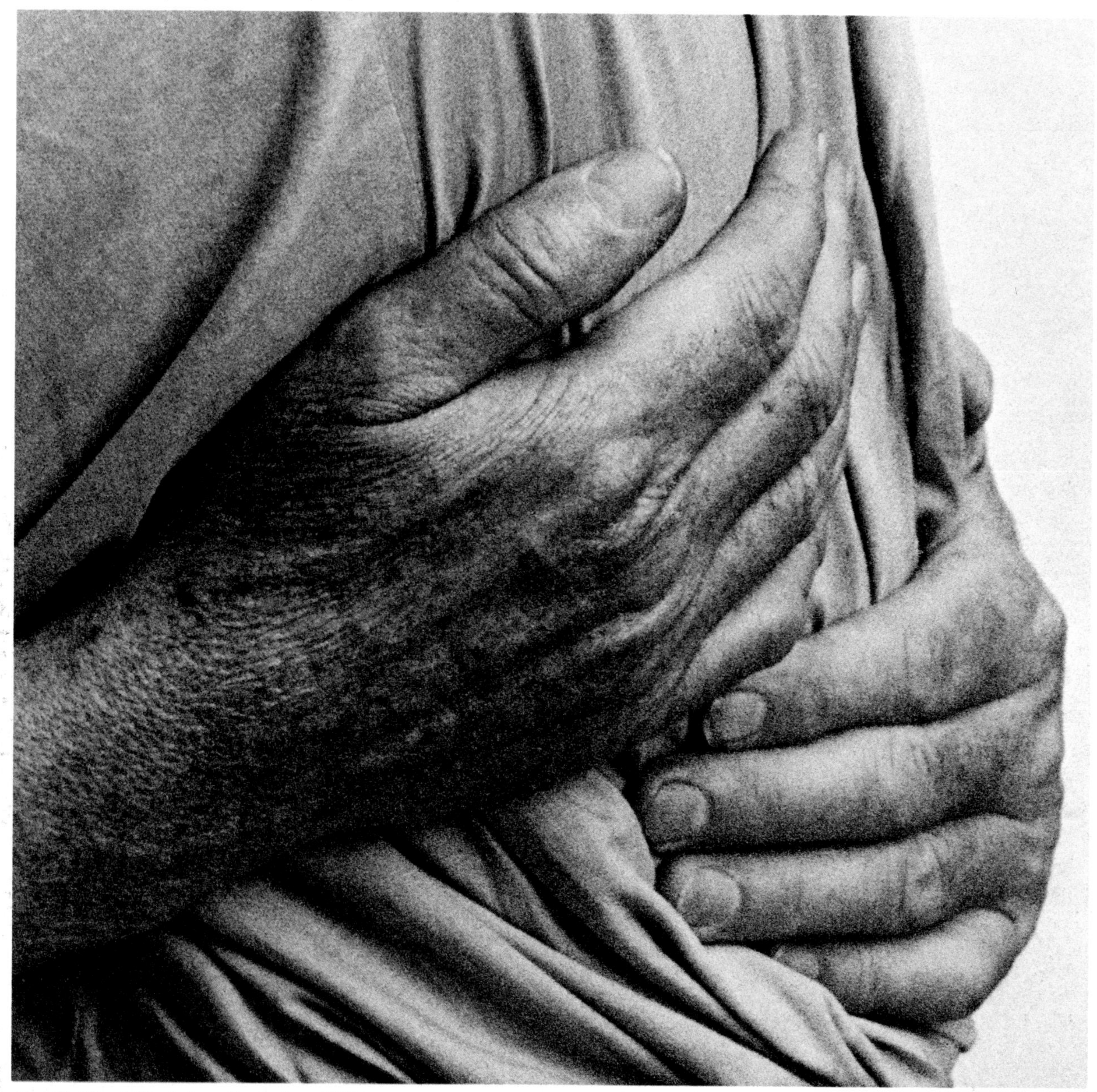

Paul's 62nd Birthday, Berkeley, 1957

I enjoy looking quietly and intently at living human beings going about their work and duties and occupations and activities as though they were spread before us for our pleasure and interest. A huge opera. A huge arena. And also to be only dimly self-aware, a figure who is part of it all, though only watching and watching. This is an exercise in vision and no finger exercise, either. For a photographer it may be closer to the final performance.

Gunlock, Utah, 1953

Nile Village, Egypt, 1963

Egypt, 1963

I wish I were a photographer. All day closed my eyes, and even so, saw things, especially the prostrate boy, lying in the street, feet up in the sun, way up, as he slept. Beautiful, sensitive, dirty feet. Asia. And the dark people, the gleaming light, move about in the world, at a different pace and rhythm, and the photographer is too busy to observe and record. Why come? Why come?

Pathan Warrior Tribesman, Khyber Pass, 1958

Nepal, 1958

*If you see mainly human misery in my photographs,
I have failed to show the multiform pattern of which it is
a reflection. For the havoc before your eyes is
the result of both natural and social forces.*

Nile Delta, Egypt, 1963

Egyptian Village, 1963

Truly marvelous. Enormous contrasts. Immense problems. Everything on great scale. The people become their land and the land becomes the people. I am one who has seen the Ganges River, the plains of central India, camel trains and countless smoky villages at suppertime and coming night. Swarming with people. Dusty and dry and wonderful color in the clothing, even in the rags that serve as clothing. Have seen the Taj Mahal by night, full moonlight. . . . The tropics, and it may be Asia, cannot be photographed on black-white film. I am confronted with doubts as to what I can grasp and record on this journey.

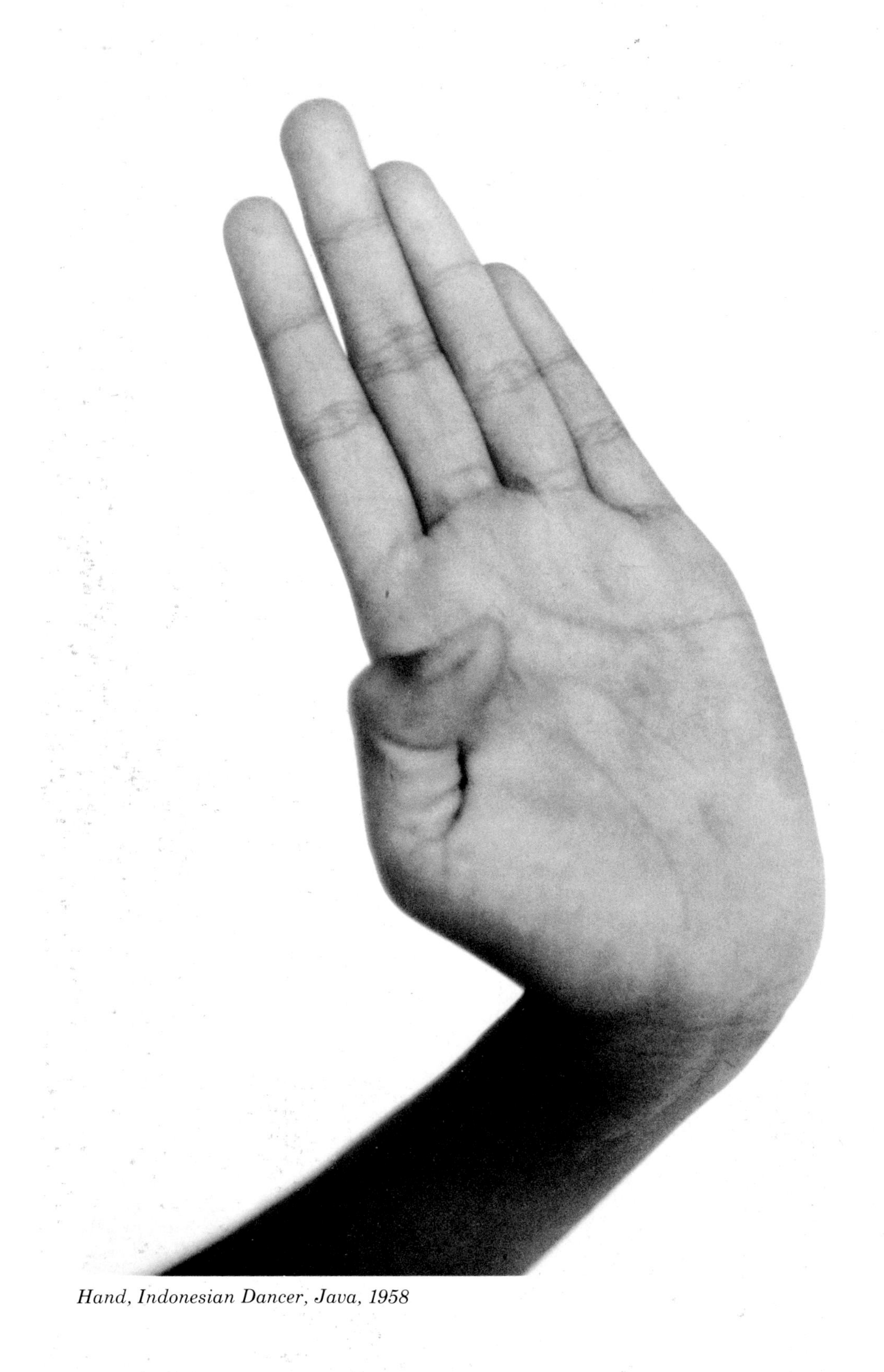

Hand, Indonesian Dancer, Java, 1958

The pageant is vast, and I clutch at tiny details, inadequate.

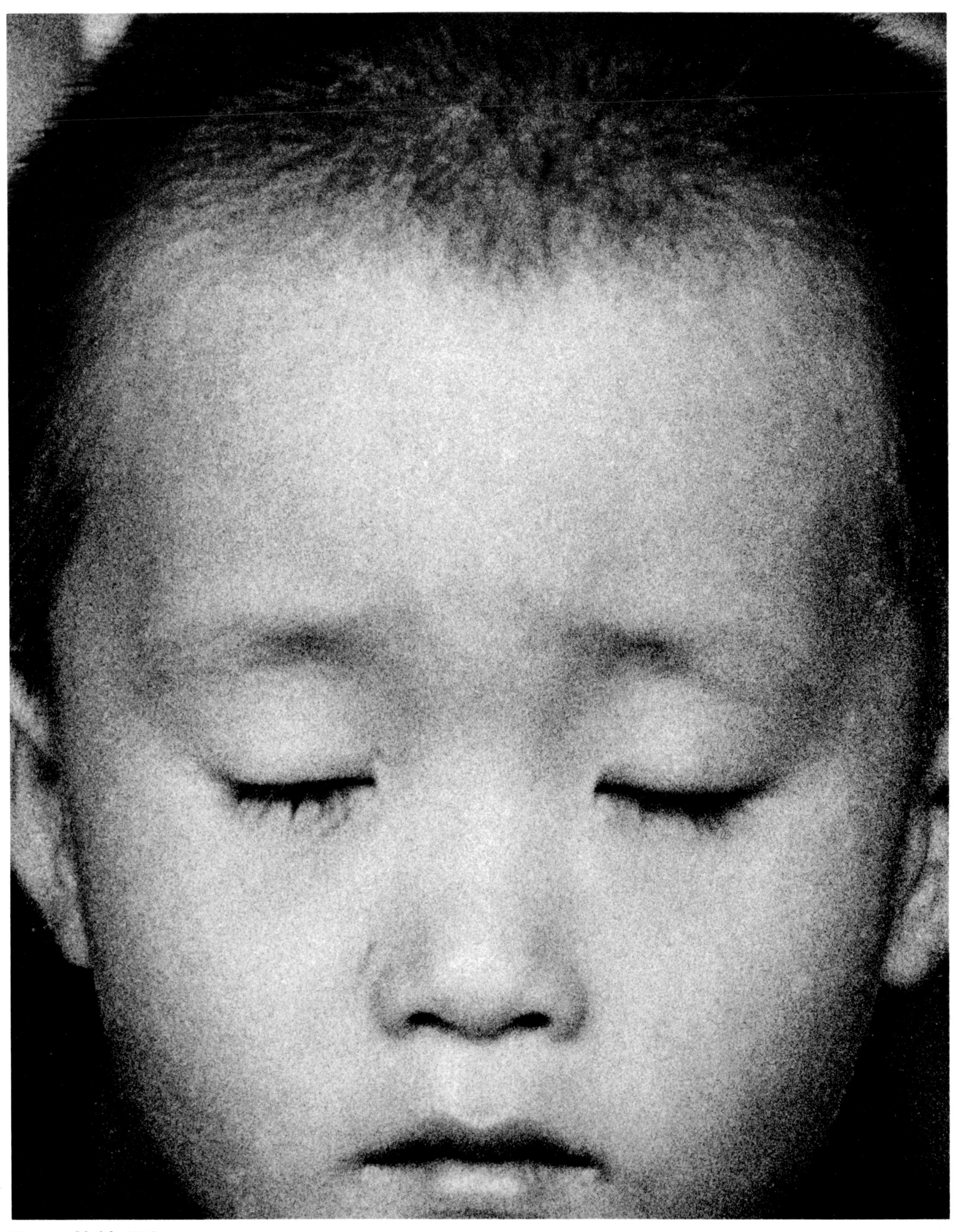

Korean Child, 1958

Berkeley, 1957

Artists are controlled by the life that beats in them, like ocean beats in on the shore. They're almost pursued;
there's something constantly acting upon them from the outside world that shapes their existence. But it isn't other artists' work, or other artists; it's what belongs to the artist. . . .

Under the Trees, 1959

Dorothea Lange, Berkeley, 1965 (Charlie Rothkin)

Afterword

Fifty years have passed since Dorothea Lange began to make the photographic record for which she is known today. For those who lived through that difficult time—a period of extreme economic dislocation that made many Americans poor for the first time—it is hard to evaluate Lange's contribution objectively. The experience is either too freshly personal or has since been eclipsed by the popular imagery of such films as *The Grapes of Wrath*. But recently we have come to appreciate that the source for the imagery—for our own visual memory of the Depression years—lies in the photographs made for the Farm Security Administration, especially in the photographs of Dorothea Lange.

Impetuous decisions appear to have impelled Lange along in her early photographic connections. She began to consider a career in photography before she had taken pictures. She followed her apprenticeship with studio photographers in New York with a studio of her own in San Francisco because she was stranded without funds. She succeeded in the stable craft of portrait work because the economy would support a wealthy middle class in their family needs for pictures. And in 1932 Lange reacted to the slump in portrait work and the nation's social upheaval by taking her camera out-of-doors.

When Lange took her camera out of her portrait studio and into the streets of San Francisco, a city populated with impoverished and homeless crowds, she carried as part of her equipment a way of working that had made her portraits particularly successful: throughout her life her best work posed a single figure, selected for stance and mood, against the crowd. *White Angel Bread Line* (1932)—by Lange's own admission her first real street picture—is a portrait of one old man carrying a cup, leaning against the barrier of a free food line. Lange's isolation of the individual dramatically personalized the plight of the group.

Lange's first Depression pictures appeared in a 1934 exhibition at the Brockhurst Street Gallery in Oakland, California. Paul Taylor, a labor economist who was writing about the same social displacement that Lange was photographing, saw the show and immediately appreciated the potential of her photographs as an interpretive tool. He recognized that social change would occur only when society was made to understand its own issues and crises, and that photography could convey the visible reality of social conditions. Soon the writer and photographer were working together for the California State Emergency Relief Administration, which preceded the Federal Farm Security Administration, traveling, photographing and interviewing throughout the South and Southwest. From the beginning of their collaboration, Lange and Taylor succeeded in moving people to help the poor. Lange's skills and insight permitted her to make photographs that required the viewer to react to a human situation: they demanded that people take action, and people did. When Lange's *Migrant Mother* (1936) appeared in newspapers, thousands sent money and offers of assistance to the work camps and clamored for California legislative support of social programs. Lange had a special kind of approach, a way of perceiving pride, strength, and the need for independence. Her pictures promised that if the poor were helped they would gladly go to work, rejoining and revitalizing a crumbling social and economic network.

Fifty years later these pictures take on new meaning because they have the appearance of truth and because they present a frightening likeness to the crisis of the 1980s—millions of unemployed and families newly poor. Lange's work may have been rejected by some of her purist contemporaries, the photographers who banded together in the Group f/64, Edward Weston, Ansel Adams, Henry Swift, and John Edwards. For them, the formal, balanced composition of a photograph was an essential part of their search for direct photographic seeing unaffected by romantic or social concerns, but Lange's concerns were not primarily the aesthetics of composition, shape, and form. Like the painters John Sloan, Edward Hopper, and Ben Shahn, who also worked for the FSA, she took as her subject people and their lives, and the record she left helped the country come to know itself. Just as today's records are now being made by television reporters and interviewers on videotape in color, Lange's pictures accurately capture America in the 1930s: people talking as their pictures are taken. They stand gray and glossy, forever frozen by the camera.

The care of such valuable documents is essential, and The Oakland Museum is fortunate to have been selected as custodian of the 35,000 negatives, prints, letters, and notes of Dorothea Lange's archive—the gift of her husband and collaborator, Paul Taylor, in 1966. The archive is a special one, not in the least because of the thorough attention to compilation and preservation on the part of the photographer and her husband. Although the FSA's policy was to retain the negatives of their photographers' work, Lange conscientiously maintained a file of her own negatives. She held back a few images from each assignment or continued to work on her own after the assignment was completed. This large collection of negatives, an alternate file to the one now held at the Library of Congress in Washington, D.C., came to Oakland as part of Taylor's gift. It offers a magnificent overview not only of Lange's work from the FSA (1935-39), but also her earlier portraits and later record of the Japanese evacuation from California during World War II, as well as her extensive foreign travel.

One of Lange's principal goals and hopes for her work was that it become available to the public in a useful form. Although outstanding prints of her work were made over the years—some of them by her friend Ansel Adams—beautiful photographic printing was not Lange's primary aim; she strived for a sense of immediacy and accuracy of documentary content. Actually, she rarely printed her work, leaving that to accomplished assistants, preferring instead to conserve her limited energy for photographing the places around her. Letters held in the Oakland collection indicate that she worried about what use might be made of her negatives and the possibility that her intentions might be altered by others, but she was also open to rethinking and by the 1960s allowed her photographs to be displayed without the interpretive captions that she labored long hours to produce in the field. Today Lange's archive makes her work available to those who wish to see and study it, and preserves it in the quality she always maintained during her lifetime.

Because the archive allows us to reinterpret our view of the past in light of the present, it has richly endowed The Oakland Museum, challenging us to gather more photographs and to preserve a record of California in the location where it can be best understood. Computers may encode massive numbers of facts, but pictures provide vital visual and graphic information—and Lange's work must be seen to have its most forceful impact. To that end The Oakland Museum holds exhibitions, such as *Celebrating a Collection: Looking at Lange Today (1975-80)* and *An American Exodus* (1976), and offers resource facilities. Since the collection is a particularly large one, it has been arranged to permit public access to a core of noted pictures, which are indexed and available in copy prints, and to allow scholars and historians to examine the entire collection in greater depth. We are especially pleased to be able to make available our resources for publication in this book, which will share Lange's photographs with an even larger public. It is our hope that Dorothea Lange's work will always be treasured as the true vision of an important part of American history.

Therese Heyman, Curator
The Oakland Museum

San Francisco, 1956

Sources

Text

Full details of the sources quoted are given in Bibliography.

PAGE

7 "You put your camera . . ." : Meltzer, p. xv.

7 "You *force* yourself . . ." : *Dorothea Lange: The Making of a Documentary Photographer,* p. 46.

9 "No one who hasn't lived . . ." : *Dorothea Lange: The Making of a Documentary Photographer,* p. 46.

9 "I was the only Gentile . . ." : *Dorothea Lange: The Making of a Documentary Photographer,* p. 13.

10 "By herself, each evening . . ." : Meltzer, p. 96.

10 "Later, she attended . . ." : Helen O'Regan to Milton Meltzer, in Meltzer, p. 15.

10 "I remember my mother . . ." : *Dorothea Lange: The Making of a Documentary Photographer,* p. 59.

10 "My mind made itself up . . ." : Daniel Dixon, "Dorothea Lange," p. 69.

11 "Among her teachers . . ." : Meltzer, p. 27.

11 " 'He knew,' she later . . ." : *Dorothea Lange: The Making of a Documentary Photographer,* p. 39.

14 "I was given a big boost . . ." : Daniel Dixon, "Dorothea Lange," p. 72.

14 "I knew I was looking . . ." : Nat Herz, "Dorothea Lange in Perspective," pp. 9–10.

15 "Dorothea Lange has turned . . ." : from Willard Van Dyke's article on Lange in *Camera Craft,* October 1934, pp. 461–67.

17 "She once confided to . . ." : *Dorothea Lange: The Making of a Documentary Photographer,* p. 122.

20 "She drove on for . . ." : Dorothea Lange, "The Assignment I'll Never Forget," pp. 42–43, 128.

20 "Many years later . . ." : Dorothea Lange to Roy Stryker, March 31, 1940, in Meltzer, p. 230.

23 "She possessed, as one friend . . ." : Jonathan Garst to Roy Stryker, November 21, 1939, in Meltzer, p. 206.

24 "We practically had to send . . ." : Roy Stryker to Richard K. Doud, interview conducted January 23, 1965, in Meltzer, p. 187.

25 "Paul Taylor is still . . ." : Garst to Stryker, November 21, 1939, in Meltzer, p. 206.

44 "Life for people . . ." : Dorothea Lange interviewed by Richard K. Doud, May 22, 1964, Archives of American Art, Detroit.

46 "For me documentary . . ." : Daniel Dixon, "Dorothea Lange," p. 69.

50 "I'd begun to get . . ." : Daniel Dixon, "Dorothea Lange," p. 75.

52 "I said, 'I will set . . .' " : Lange interviewed by Richard K. Doud, May 22, 1964, Archives of American Art, Detroit.

56 "It's a very difficult . . ." : *Dorothea Lange: The Making of a Documentary Photographer,* p. 46.

60 "They looked very woebegone . . ." : Lange interviewed by Richard K. Doud, May 22, 1964, Archives of American Art, Detroit.

62 "Their roots were . . ." : Meltzer, p. 97.

68 "You know, so often . . ." : Lange interviewed by Richard K. Doud, May 22, 1964, Archives of American Art, Detroit.

72 "I can only say . . ." : Nat Herz, "Dorothea Lange in Perspective," pp. 9–10.

76 "It was raining . . ." : Dorothea Lange, "The Assignment I'll Never Forget," pp. 42–43, 128.

80 "Woman of the high plains . . ." : *Dorothea Lange Looks at the American Country Woman,* p. 28.

84 "Earlier, I'd gotten . . ." : Daniel Dixon, "Dorothea Lange," pp. 72, 138.

94 "Accidentally learned . . ." : Meltzer, pp. 198–9.

101 "Ma Burnham . . ." : *Dorothea Lange Looks at the American Country Woman,* p. 66.

103 "These are women of the . . ." : *Dorothea Lange Looks at the American Country Woman,* p. 13.

104 "Early Californian . . ." : *Dorothea Lange Looks at the American Country Woman,* p. 14.

108 "A documentary photograph . . ." : *Dorothea Lange: The Making of a Documentary Photographer,* pp. 155–58.

114 "Sometimes you stick around . . ." : Lange interviewed by Richard K. Doud, Archives of American Art, Detroit.

116 "I had begun to talk . . ." : Meltzer, p. 97.

120 "I have a wife . . ." : Meltzer, p. 174.

121 "None of us vote . . ." : Meltzer, p. 174.

124 "Documentary photography records . . ." : Suzanne Riess and Malca Chall, *Paul Schuster Taylor: California Social Scientist,* v. 1, p. 238A.

127 "Everything is propaganda . . ." : *Dorothea Lange: The Making of a Documentary Photographer,* p. 49.

131 "Well, I many times . . ." : Lange interviewed by Richard K. Doud, Archives of American Art, Detroit.

132 "What I photographed . . ." : *Dorothea Lange: The Making of a Documentary Photographer,* pp. 186, 187, 194.

138 "Woman of the Far West . . ." : *Dorothea Lange Looks at the American Country Woman,* p. 62.

140 "Toquerville is . . ." : *Dorothea Lange Looks at the American Country Woman,* p. 140.

140 "Home place . . ." : *Dorothea Lange Looks at the American Country Woman,* p. 64.

141 "On the floor . . ." : Dorothea Lange and Pirkle Jones, "Death of a Valley," p. 146.

142 "All photographs . . ." : *Dorothea Lange: The Making of a Documentary Photographer,* pp. 205–6.

146 "I find that it . . ." : *Dorothea Lange Looks at the American Country Woman,* pp. 9, 90.

152 "To know ahead . . ." : *Dorothea Lange: The Making of a Documentary Photographer,* pp. 177–78.

158 "I enjoy looking . . ." : Meltzer, p. 335.

161 "I wish I were . . ." : Lange's travel diary, December 22, 1958, Dorothea Lange Collection, Oakland Museum.

165 "Truly marvelous . . ." : Meltzer, p. 321.

166 "The pageant is vast . . ." : Meltzer, p. 322.

168 "Artists are controlled . . ." : *Dorothea Lange: The Making of a Documentary Photographer,* p. 23.

Photographs

The works reproduced in *Dorothea Lange: Photographs of a Lifetime* are courtesy of the Dorothea Lange Collection, Oakland Museum, copyright © 1978 The City of Oakland, except as follows: page 13 top and bottom left, The Brigham Young University Collection; page 16 left, Rondal Partridge; right, Helen Dixon; page 17, Rondal Partridge; page 23, Helen Dixon; page 35, Wayne Miller; page 40 top and bottom left, Helen Dixon; top right, Rondal Partridge; bottom, Shirley C. Burden; page 41, Pirkle Jones; page 42, Rondal Partridge; page 43, Richard Conrat; pages 18 left, 19, 22 left, 24, 25 right, 26, 27, 28, 29, 31, 32, 33, 51, 63, 69, 71, 73, 75, 78, 82, 85, 88, 96, 100, 112, 114, 116, 117, 125, The Library of Congress, Washington, D.C.; page 141, Pirkle Jones; and page 170, Charlie Rothkin.

Chronology

1895

MAY 25. Born Dorothea Margaretta Nutzhorn in Hoboken, New Jersey, to Joanna Lange and Henry Nutzhorn. Her maternal ancestors emigrated from Stuttgart (c. 1860s).

1899

Family moves to Weehawken, New Jersey.

1901

Dorothea's brother, Henry Martin Nutzhorn, born in Weehawken.

1902

Contracts poliomyelitis, which leaves her with a lifelong limp. At sixty-five, comments: "It was perhaps the most important thing that happened to me. [It] formed me, guided me, instructed me, helped me, and humiliated me. All those things at once. I've never gotten over it and I am aware of the force and power of it."

1907

Henry Nutzhorn abandons his family. Dorothea, her mother, and brother return to Hoboken to live with maternal grandmother, Sophie Vottler Lange, and great-aunt Caroline.

To support family, Joanna Lange works in a branch of the New York Public Library on Manhattan's Lower East Side.

Dorothea enrolled at P.S. 62, one of few Gentiles among some 3,000 Jewish children. Becomes acutely aware of cultural variations. Is unhappy in the intellectually competitive school atmosphere. Takes long walks alone on the Lower East Side. Spends time reading in library where her mother works. Studies all kinds of pictures, pinning the best she finds to her wall.

1908

Greatly affected by Isadora Duncan, whose performances she attends at the Metropolitan Opera House.

1909

Enters Wadleigh High School for Girls on Manhattan's Upper West Side. Majors in Latin, which she barely passes. Receives her highest grades—in the 80s—in English, drawing, and music.

Home life miserable because of tyrannical, hard-drinking grandmother. Dorothea becomes, in her words, "solitary and rebellious" and spends as much time as possible away from home. Begins friendship with Florence Ahlstrom. With Florence, begins to cut classes in order to walk New York's streets and parks, and to attend free concerts and visit theaters and museums.

1913

Graduates from high school and announces decision to become a photographer, although she has never owned a camera or taken a picture. Joanna Lange leaves library job and begins work as juvenile court investigator. Dorothea accompanies her mother on nighttime interviews. Because of family objections to her choice of a career, she attends New York Training School for Teachers [later Teacher's College, Columbia University]. Attends classes daily but spends spare moments working in photographers' studios. Later in life says: "My mind made itself up. It just came to me that photography would be a good thing for me to do. I thought at the time I could earn my living at it without too much difficulty. I'd make modest photographs of people, starting with the people whom I knew. I had never owned a camera, but I just knew that that was what I wanted to do."

1914

Impressed by Arnold Genthe's photographs of Isadora Duncan on exhibit at Genthe's Fifth Avenue studio, applies for a job, which she gets. Each afternoon after school works in Genthe's studio, the youngest of three women on his staff, as receptionist, making proofs, spotting, retouching, and mounting photographs. Genthe presents her with her first camera and offers critical evaluations of her work over next year or so. Begins to photograph children on her own. Quits teacher-training school.

1915-16

Leaves Genthe's studio. Works for Aram Kazanjian for six months and learns how to run a portrait studio. Moves on to Mrs. A. Spencer-Beatty's studio, where she is given first opportunity to use a camera professionally after regular photographer quits. Earns twelve dollars a week. Photographs many prominant subjects.

Meets itinerant photographer, first in a succession of unofficial teachers. Agrees to let him use as darkroom old chicken coop in back of house, which they clean and refurbish together. He teaches her various old-fashioned photographic techniques and how to develop her negatives. Charles H. Davis, formerly a successful portrait photographer, shows her how to pose models and shares his experience.

1917

Takes basic photography seminar (about ten students) given by Clarence H. White at Columbia University, but does not complete any assignments. When class ends, buys a large camera and two lenses. Working by herself day and night takes portraits of her family, friends, and strangers—especially children.

Introduced to work of Karl Struss, Baron de Meyer, Paul Outerbridge, and, perhaps, Gertrude Käsebier, Margaret Bourke-White, Doris Ulmann, Laura Gilpin—all part of Clarence White's circle and/or former students of his. Desire to make portraits grows.

1918

JANUARY. Leaves New York permanently as a test of independence and strength, hoping to work her way around the world to China as a photographer. With Florence Ahlstrom, two suitcases, and $140, and against family objections, sails to New Orleans, then on to El Paso, New Mexico, and Los Angeles, arriving five months after original departure in San Francisco, where a pickpocket leaves the two young women with less than five dollars.

Because of previous experience as a darkroom assistant, hired as an over-the-counter photo-finisher at March & Company, a dry goods and photo supply house on Market Street. Joins camera club on Market Street for darkroom privileges. Through job meets Roi Partridge, Imogen Cunningham, and Consuela Kanaga. In West, assumes mother's maiden name, Lange.

1919

Within months of arrival in San Francisco, receives two offers to be underwritten in own portrait business. Opens portrait studio in the rear of Hill-Tollerton Print Room at 540 Sutter Street, where she stays until 1925. Meets with immediate success, photographing wealthy, influential, largely Jewish San Francisco families at the studio and in subjects' homes. All work done on commission; does no personal photography. Begins to date all photographs.

Says later, "I didn't do anything phenomenal. I wasn't trying to . . . . Good meant to me being useful, filling a need, really pleasing the people for whom I was working . . . My personal interpretation was second to the need of the other fellow."

Partridge introduces Lange to Maynard Dixon, at forty-five an established artist and illustrator.

1920

MARCH 21. Lange and Dixon marry, move to 1080 Broadway, on Russian Hill. Dixon's ten-year-old daughter, Constance, joins them. Active artistic life among bohemian circles, including Cunningham and Partridge, Ed Borein, Ralph Stackpole, Gottardo Piazzoni, Gertrude Albright, Fremont Older, Charles Erskine, Scott Wood, Sara Bard Field, Lucien Labaudt, Timothy Pflueger, Albert Bender.

1921

With mother, new step-father, and Constance, accompanies Dixon on sketching trip to the High Sierras. Dixon makes frequent trips, with Dorothea or alone.

1922

With Dixon visits Navajo reservation in Arizona. Photographs while Dixon sketches. Shocked at mistreatment of Indians by the government.

1923

Travels to East Coast to develop market for Dixon's paintings. Gallery owner Robert Macbeth is enthusiastic and succeeds in promoting shows in Philadelphia, Pittsburgh, Cleveland, Cincinnati, and Washington, D.C.

Extended trip to Navajo and Hopi country with California millionaire Anita Baldwin McClaughry. Lange photographs; Dixon paints.

1925

MAY 15. Daniel Rhodes Dixon is born.

1926

Dixon travels to Arizona to paint. Family moves to 1607 Taylor Street.

1928

JUNE 12. John Eaglefeather Dixon is born. Dixon travels to Sacramento to paint mural in State Library. Working closely with laborers he develops what he calls a "union" feeling.

Family life stormy because of temperamental differences, continual separations during Dixon's trips, and tension between Lange and her stepdaughter, Constance. Twenty-five-year age gap and Dixon's poor health (emphysema and tuberculosis) are tremendous strains.

c. 1928

Sets up studio at 802 Montgomery Street—the crossroads of Chinatown, the Barbary Coast, the wholesale district, and the financial district—where she remains for about three years.

1929

Family travels again to Arizona. Dixon completes mural "Legend of Earth and Sun," for the Arizona Biltmore Hotel, in Phoenix.

Later that summer, family travels to California gold country, where Lange senses impending move into documentary photography.

In fall, family returns to San Francisco.

1930s

Stock market crash decreases commissions for both Lange and Dixon. For duration of the Depression, children board with a family in Watsonville.

1930

Dixon travels to Tehachapi Mountains and edge of Mojave Desert to work.

Roger Sturtevant sublets Lange's studio.

1930–31

During drive to Taos, New Mexico, Dixon turns over car; Lange forbids him to drive family again. Spends seven months at Ranchos de Taos, where Dixon lent studio by Mabel Dodge Luhan. Lange influenced by Paul Strand's presence in the area, though does little photographic work. Occupies most of time with duties of wife and mother.

Returns to San Francisco. To save money, Lange lives at her studio and Dixon in his, three doors down on Montgomery Street.

1932–33

Continues to make portraits for diminishing clientele. Portraits more sharply focused, dry-mounted on white board without embellishment. Depression and uncertain financial future seriously affect work patterns.

Family summers at Fallen Leaf Lake near Lake Tahoe. Lange returns to San Francisco and sends out advertisement for "Pictures of People—Season of 1932–1933."

Makes *White Angel Bread Line*.

Photographs street demonstrations and May Day. Continues to do portraits to finance her developing documentary work.

Becomes acquainted with Group f/64, but is not asked to participate in their activities; Group f/64 more interested in aesthetics of photography than in Lange's social direction.

Approached by Communists, but does not join them.

Family travels to Utah.

1934

Dixons move to 2515 Gough Street. Lange gives up studio and works at home. Dixon goes to Boulder Dam to paint, supported by the Public Works of Art Project.

Photographs maritime strike.

At the suggestion of Edward Weston, Willard Van Dyke exhibits Lange in Oakland Studio (Annie Brigman's former studio) at 983 Brockhurst Street.

Visits Fallen Leaf with Dixon in late summer.

Paul S. Taylor, labor economist at the University of California, sees Brockhurst exhibition and phones Lange to discuss her photographs. Uses one of her maritime pictures in the article "San Francisco and the General Strike," in September 1934 *Survey Graphic* with credit line "Photograph by Dorothea Lange, San Francisco."

OCTOBER. Willard Van Dyke's critical article on Lange's work appears in *Camera Craft*.

NOVEMBER. Van Dyke arranges party of photographers (himself, Imogen Cunningham, Preston Holder, Mary Jeanette Edwards), including Lange, to accompany Taylor to photograph the Unemployed Exchange Association's sawmill cooperative near Oroville. First meeting of Lange and Taylor. Some of these photographhcs used by Taylor in an exhibition at University of California.

Decides that independent photography is only course to pursue.

DECEMBER. Second exhibition of Lange's work held at the public library branch on Vallejo Street, San Francisco.

1935

FEBRUARY. Joins Paul Taylor's staff at California's State Emergency Relief Administration (SERA), Division of Rural Rehabilitation, where she works through June. Listed on table of organization as "clerk-stenographer," since no slot exists for photographer (position was Taylor's idea). Witnesses sudden influx of poverty-stricken migrants into California. Covers entire state including Marysville, Yuba City, Nipomo, Sacramento, Stockton, Napa, Bakersfield, Fresno. Photographs support Taylor text recommending camps for migratory workers. Taylor-Lange report appeals for $100,000 to initiate program; $20,000 is final amount authorized.

APRIL. California, New Mexico, including Texas, Claud, Bosque, Lordsburg and Deming.

MAY. California and New Mexico.

JUNE. California with particular emphasis on San Francisco.

Roy E. Stryker brought from Columbia University, New York, to Washington, D.C., by Rexford Guy Tugwell to write a history of resettlement. Instead, Stryker sets up photographic division of the newly created Resettlement Administration (RA) to do reporting on specific New Deal programs. After only a few weeks on the job sees Lange's photographs made for California agency. Pare Lorentz also sees the Taylor-Lange reports; inspired by her photographs, includes California sequence in the *The Plow That Broke the Plains* (released 1936). Lange works with him on film for one week.

AUGUST 21. Lange receives telegram from Lawrence Hewes asking if she will accept Resettlement Administration job if offered. Agrees to transfer from California SERA to Roy Stryker's unit of the RA.

SEPTEMBER 1. Hired by Stryker as Photographer-Investigator "EO-8" (Western Regional Office), stationed at Berkeley. Salary $2,300 a year. Joins Arthur Rothstein, Ben Shahn as staff photographer. (Works full-time for RA until 1937, at which time it becomes the Farm Security Administration; from 1937 until 1939 works part-time; and then occasionally until 1942. The unit is transferred to the Office of War Information in 1943.) Given first assignment under Stryker to record migratory families moving from Great Plains to California at new federal camp at Marysville, which an earlier Taylor-Lange report had helped establish. Begins to talk with subjects. Taylor appointed Regional Labor Advisor to RA, assigned to same office. Begins close working and personal relationship with Taylor.

OCTOBER–NOVEMBER. The Taylor and Dixon families spend Thanksgiving together in Nevada where Dixon and Mrs. Taylor are getting divorces.

DECEMBER 6. Marries Paul Taylor in Albuquerque, New Mexico. Wedding trip becomes working holiday. Taylor brings three children with him to marriage: Katharine, thirteen years old; Ross, ten; Margot, six. Family rents home at 2706 Virginia Street, Berkeley.

By year's end RA staff consists of Arthur Rothstein, Carl Mydans, Walker Evans, Ben Shahn, and Dorothea Lange. Frustrated by distance from Washington and fact she cannot keep her negatives or control quality of prints, builds darkroom/studio at home to develop and print her own RA material. When Ansel Adams makes trip to East Coast, Lange enlists him to meet Stryker and plead her case to print own negatives. Adams persuades Stryker to let Lange print own negatives, but Stryker insists they then be sent to Washington with three prints.

1936

FEBRUARY. California and San Francisco.

MARCH. California and Utah, including the towns of Price, Witsoe, Escalante and Carbon County. Makes *Migrant Mother* pictures. Two images appear in *San Francisco News* along with story that federal government is sending 20,000 pounds of food to hungry migrants.

APRIL. Receives numerous requests for pictures of migratory labor from press services, newspapers, and magazines. Utah. Paul Taylor transferred in late spring to research division of Social Security Board. Taylor and Lange continue team work in the field.

MAY. Lange makes first trip East to Washington, D.C., assigned to Eastern region for summer. Finds warmth and support at Central office. New Jersey, including Hightstown, Bridgeton and Millville. In Hightstown, New Jersey, Lange documents RA projects to resettle unemployed families of New York City garment workers; one of the few times Lange works with FSA colleagues, in this instance Ben Shahn, Edwin Rosskam, and Arthur Rothstein.

Taylor works at Washington office of Social Security Board.

JUNE. Mississippi, including Clarksdale, Hill House, Coahoma County, Cleveland, Leland, Greenville, Yazoo City, Washington County, Foote, Hinds County, Issaquena County, Vicksburg, Piney Woods, Brookhaven, Hazelhurst, Jackson, Hancock County, Kiln; Alabama, including Anniston, Eden, Birmingham, Eutaw.

The Plow That Broke the Plains released.

Meets Aaron Siskind, young member of the Photo League, who shows her work from the League's *Harlem Document,* a photographic project documenting daily life in Harlem.

SUMMER. *U.S. Camera* invites Lange to submit *Migrant Mother* to annual show of outstanding photographs, the first exhibition that recognizes FSA photographers. Washington wants to make the prints but Lange objects and wins right to borrow negatives to make her own print. Signs her name to this print which travels nationally and internationally.

Walker Evans and James Agee, and Margaret Bourke-White and Erskine Caldwell begin collaborating on their respective books: *Let Us Now Praise Famous Men* (Agee and Evans), and *You Have Seen Their Faces* (White and Caldwell).

Arkansas, including Seligman, Mountain Home, Fayetteville, Fort Smith, Russellville, Judsonia, Conway, Little Rock, England, Lake Dick, Earle, Memphis, Blythville; Mississippi, Alabama, Georgia, including Hartwell, Green County, Social Circle, Atlanta, Thomaston, Musella, Cordale, Americus, Marshallville, Macon County, Hazelhurst, Homerville, Waycross, DuPont, Valdosta; Pennsylvania, including Washington; Indiana, including Clayton and Indianapolis.

JULY. Lange experiences Depression in South. In North she felt the Depression had "shaken apart any form of social order," but in the South she finds the social order (i.e., black and white, rich and poor) remains firm.

AUGUST. California, San Francisco, Arizona, including Glendale, Phoenix, Chandler, Tombstone, Duncan, Blythe, Yuma; New Mexico, Texas, including Brownsville, Corpus Christi, San Antonio, Carrizo Springs, Austin, Bryan, Bell County, Waco, Ellis County, Marshall, Dallas, Stanton, Odessa, Anton, Lubbock, Wichita Falls, Childress, Carey, Hardeman County, Memphis, Goodlet, Hall County, Dalhart, Perryton; Oklahoma, including Cimarron County, Texas County, Claremore, Muskogee County, Sequoyak County, Webber's Falls, Sallisaw, Cleveland County, Oklahoma City, Oklahoma County, McAlester, Krebs, Chicksha, Comanche County, Mangum, Austee Cachr, Oil City, McCurtain County, Eagletown, Idabel, Caddo; Arkansas.

FALL. Lange returns home with 17,000 miles behind her. Pressured by getting material from cross-country trip to Stryker.

SEPTEMBER. "Classic" *Migrant Mother* printed in *Survey Graphic,* full-page credit to RA and Lange. Same issue has article by Taylor, with four other Lange photographs, about federal agencies meeting the needs of migrants.

Photographs in California.

OCTOBER. Dropped from RA payroll, because of federal budget cuts. Stryker encourages Lange to accept other jobs. Works on per diem basis for RA and does private documentary work. Photographs lettuce pickers' strikes in Salinas.

College Art Association travels 110 RA photographs around country, including Lange pictures.

Receives first request from *Life* magazine for story on migratory labor.

Works in California.

While on the road Lange and Taylor farm out combined family of five children among three families they know. At home Lange "harnessed to the house—not a liberated woman." Family competes with her work, except in summers, when children are placed so parents can work. Struggles keeping up with difficult teenage children; torn between family and career. First symptoms of ulcer show up.

1937

JANUARY 23. Rehired by RA. Put in charge of compilation of photographs to illustrate Senate's Lubin report on migrant labor.

WINTER–SPRING. Plans and prepares exhibits, reports, and lay-outs for newspapers and magazines. First trip during this period to Imperial Valley, where RA has not yet extended funds. Again encounters exploitation and control of migrants by landowners. Bosses reportedly employ Red-scare tactics to quell strikes and worker unrest.

Archibald MacLeish looks at RA photographs for inspiration on his poem about areas and communities used and then abandoned by industry. Lange photographs Tombstone, New Mexico, once a thriving mining town, now desolate, with MacLeish's book in mind.

MARCH. California, San Francisco, Arizona/California state line.

APRIL. California.

MAY. Travels in Southwest again, to Arizona and New Mexico, covering tenancy in south Texas, central Texas, Oklahoma, Arkansas, down to Mississippi, Alabama, and Georgia. RA now doing work, off the record, for Department of Agriculture, at request of Secretary Henry A. Wallace. Wallace concerned about cricket scourge devastating parts of Utah, Nevada, and Wyoming. Lange goes there to photograph.

Taylor's twelve-year-old son, Ross, accompanies them on southern trip, which for most part follows spontaneous route. Encounters heavy rains in north Texas; sees flood refugees for first time. Observes people heading in both directions on highway, some leaving California to return east, some just beginning arduous trip west. Photographs men she and Taylor interview in north Texas. Learns about bureaucratic problems of federal relief programs.

JUNE. Moves from Texas into Oklahoma, Arkansas, Tennessee, including Blythville, Wilson and Memphis; Louisiana, including Shreveport, Fullerton, New Orleans; Mississippi, Georgia, South Carolina, including Chesnee and Gaffney.

Mails negatives to Washington to be processed and evaluated by Stryker. He returns them in groupings, always noting that she can alter his decisions to coordinate with her themes.

Letter from Stryker notes criticism RA has received for focussing only on hardship cases. Asks Lange to photograph successful farms and cotton-picking season.

JULY. Louisiana, Mississippi, Florida, including Caryville; Georgia, South Carolina.

LATE SUMMER. Taylor and Lange return home. RA changed to Farm Security Administration (FSA) under jurisdiction of Department of Agriculture. Stryker's history section charged with carrying out the functions of Bankhead-Jones Farm Tenancy Act, which work of Taylor and Lange helped bring about.

Pare Lorentz produces *The River* for FSA.

OCTOBER. Along with Walker Evans, again loses RA job after federal budget cuts. Arthur Rothstein and Russell Lee only photographers with permanent positions. Spends time until official termination grouping prints and organizing captions.

You Have Seen Their Faces, by Margaret Bourke-White and novelist husband, Erskine Caldwell, published. FSA photographers and writers outraged at what they consider Bourke-White's largely fictitious depiction of migrant laborers.

1938

Lange spends early part of year getting organized and trying to see field work from point of view of private citizen. Suggests ideas to Stryker but no assignment materializes. Continues to work privately and on regional duty.

Migrant Mother image assimilated in lithograph to represent *The Spanish Mother, Terror of 1938* during Spanish Civil War.

JANUARY–APRIL. Works in California.

MARCH. Taylor testifies before Special Senate Committee on Unemployment and Relief. Uses report illustrated with Lange photographs.

MacLeish's book *Land of the Free* published. Of eighty-eight photographs in the book, thirty-three are by Lange. Complimentary copies sent to influential people in Washington. Pare Lorentz, in *Saturday Review of Literature,* writes, "I give [Lange] chief credit for putting on celluloid what Mr. MacLeish failed to put in words."

Taylor and Lange plan third summer field trip together. Only agreement she can make with Stryker is for FSA to purchase selected group of one hundred negatives at three dollars each. Purchases a Zeiss Jewell View camera with a convertible Protar Lens.

Since Lange is not on FSA payroll, assignments come to Taylor from Social Security Board.

JUNE 1. Leaves on field trip: starts at southern tip of California, to Arizona, New Mexico into Texas Panhandle, down to Mississippi, South Carolina, and Georgia. From deep South heads northwest to Missouri, Arkansas, and Oklahoma.

Decides to have Ansel Adams develop negatives from trip.

EARLY JULY. Spends one week in Washington, D.C. Stryker's superiors no longer see usefulness of documentary photography in FSA work, and recommend further cutbacks. Lange begins to think about a picture-text collaboration with Taylor.

Marion Post Wolcott joins FSA team; only other woman hired.

JULY. Georgia.

AUGUST. Arkansas, Missouri, Mississippi.

SEPTEMBER 29. Returns to FSA payroll at previous salary of $2,300. Receives notification while in hospital recovering from appendectomy.

OCTOBER. Works in southern California with assignment from regional supervisor, Fred Soule, to cover life in the camps and FSA projects. Begins to think about other subjects and starts work for series on California town and city life.

FSA shares in International Photographic Exhibition arranged by Willard Morgan at the Grand Palace. The Museum of Modern Art in New York mounts FSA section from the show and tours it throughout the country.

U.S. Camera annual devotes 32 pages to FSA.

Lange and Taylor begin intensive work on book, *An American Exodus,* which continues through spring of 1939. Rents nearby attic workspace for fifteen dollars a month.

DECEMBER. California.

1939
EARLY YEAR. Assigned to cover California. (Rothstein, Lee, and Wolcott dispersed to South and Midwest).

New Democratic government in California developing New Deal aid programs.

FEBRUARY–MAY. Goes into field again. Reports on spreading pattern of industrialized agriculture. Encounters overabundance of labor.

APRIL. John Steinbeck's *The Grapes of Wrath* published. Immediate best seller as public takes fictional work to be factual depiction of migrant life. Within two months Twentieth Century-Fox purchases film rights. Director John Ford uses Lange's photographs as primary research source. Praising work of Lange and Steinbeck, Pare Lorentz writes, "Lange, with her still pictures . . . and Steinbeck, with two novels, a play, and a motion picture, have done more for these tragic nomads than all the politicians of the country."

JULY. Works for summer in North Carolina, including Olive Hill, Roxboro, Gordontown, Orange County, Hillsborough, Cedar Grove, Mebane, Person County, Granville County, Oxford, Shoofly, Durham County, Morrisville, Upchurch, Wake County, Pittsboro, Chatham County, Siler City, Randolph County; also New York.

Joins Taylor in New York to make rounds of publishers with their book. Reynal and Hitchcock agree to publish, setting year's end as publication date.

EARLY AUGUST. Returns to Berkeley. Oregon, including Pendleton, Umatilla County, Baker County, Pleasant Valley, Durkee, Dead Ox Flat, Ontario, Nyssa, Homedale, Ouryhee Reservoir, Willowcreek, Vale, Cow Hollow, Merrill, Klamath Falls, Gilchrist, Josephine County, Grants Pass, Eugene, Corvallis, Independence, Stayton, Salem, Marion County, Yamhill County, Polk County, Portland; Washington, including Quincy, Grant County, Toppenish, Yakima County, Lewis County, Tenino, Centralia, Thurston County, Michigan Hill, Vader, Elma, Malone Grays Harbor County.

SEPTEMBER. Lange and Taylor worry that outbreak of war in Europe may hinder publication of *An American Exodus.*

Although Stryker has reservations about Lange publishing photographs he believes to be government property, he feels the circulation of photographs important and orders special paper for prints.

OCTOBER. Lange works in Northwest: Oregon; home, then returns to Northwest with plans to go on to Wyoming, Utah, and Nevada; Idaho, including Bonners Ferry, Boundary County, Bonner County, Gem County. While in Oregon, Stryker telephones to notify Lange she will be dropped from FSA on January 1.

Pare Lorentz requests Lange be assigned to aid on the production of his film *The Land.* Nothing comes of request.

1940
JANUARY. *An American Exodus* published. Reviews are generally favorable.

Bouts begin with a series of difficult illnesses. Ulcers do not receive proper treatment. Does special assignments for the U.S. Bureau of Agricultural Economics. Moves from Virginia Street to Euclid Avenue, Berkeley.

MARCH. Department of Anthropology and Sociology, University of Oklahoma, mounts exhibition of forty-nine photographs by Russell Lee, Dorothea Lange, Arthur Rothstein and Ben Shahn.

1940–41
DECEMBER 31–JANUARY 12. Work is exhibited for the first time at The Museum of Modern Art. *Migrant Mother* included in a show of recent acquisitions.

1941
Awarded a Guggenheim fellowship, the first woman to receive a photography grant. Starts study of cooperative societies in the United States: Hutterites, Amana Society, Shakers—which she never completes.

1942
Works for the War Relocation Authority (WRA) photographing Japanese-Americans being evacuated from the Pacific coast to internment camps as a result of Executive Order 9066.

Roy Stryker hires Paul Vanderbilt to organize FSA file indexed by subject for historical purposes (272,000 negatives); 150,000 mounted prints transferred to Prints and Photographs Division of the Library of Congress.

1943–45
Works for Office of War Information from New York. (Negatives lost between New York and Washington.) All government negatives from these years lost in transit.

Works with Ansel Adams on story for *Fortune* ("Richmond, California—The City with the Purple Heart"). Photographs for Office of War Information.

Ulcer attacks, last through 1946.

1945
APRIL 25–JUNE 26. Photographs the United Nations Conference in San Francisco for State Department. Afterward, becomes ill and remains in Berkeley, relatively inactive until 1950.

c. 1949
Meets Edward Steichen.

1951
Begins to photograph actively again.

SEPTEMBER 26–OCTOBER 6. Participates in photo conference at Aspen, Colorado, also attended by Ansel Adams, Barbara Morgan, Beaumont and Nancy Newhall, and Minor White.

1952–53
NOVEMBER 26–MARCH 1. Thirty-six photographs included in *Diogenes with a Camera,* Edward Steichen's exhibition at The Museum of Modern Art, New York.

Helps found *Aperture,* a quarterly publication of photography, with Ansel Adams, Barbara Morgan, Beaumont Newhall, Nancy Newhall, Ernest Lovie, Melton Ferris, Dody Warren, and Minor White.

1953
Works with Ansel Adams and her writer son, Daniel Dixon, in Utah on assignment for *Life* ("Three Mormon Towns," September 6, 1954).

1954
Goes to Ireland with Daniel Dixon on assignment for *Life* ("The Irish Country People," March 21, 1955).

Works sporadically. Photographs mainly in Oakland. Begins work on several photo essays in California: "The Public Defender," "On Security," and "On Justice." Becomes Edward Steichen's West Coast representative to review portfolios for *The*

Family of Man exhibition. Selects work with Shirley C. Burden, then sends negatives and prints to New York.

1955

JANUARY 26–MAY 8. Nine photographs included in *The Family of Man* at The Museum of Modern Art.

Teaches at San Francisco Art Institute. Her darkroom and field assistants during this period include Ron Partridge, Ralph Gibson, Zoe Brown, and Richard Conrat.

1956–57

Photographs the devastation of the Berryessa Valley with Pirkle Jones for essay *Death of a Valley* (*Aperture,* 1960).

1957

First seminar at California School of Fine Arts [now San Francisco Art Institute].

Weekends at cabin, acquired in 1955, at Steep Ravine, twenty miles north of San Francisco in Marin County.

1958–59

Gives several critiques and one seminar at the School of Fine Arts, where she is also a member of informal advisory group until 1962.

JUNE–JANUARY. Accompanies Taylor in Asia and Europe (Kabul, Tashkent, Moscow, Stuttgart, Rotterdam, London), where he is consultant to U.S.–International Cooperation Administration. Also travels in Korea, Japan, Hong Kong, Thailand, Singapore, Rangoon, Calcutta, Nepal. Lange photographs as opportunity affords.

1960–64

Plans new projects. Works on *The American Country Woman.* Concentrates on photographing family and home life. Despite frequent bouts of illness, travels abroad with Taylor.

1960

Goes to Venezuela and Ecuador with Taylor, who is studying agrarian reform and community development for the United Nations.

"*La Donna Rurale Americana di Dorothea Lange*" exhibited at the Biblioteca Communale in Milan, Italy.

1961

MARCH. Solo exhibition at the Carl Siembab Gallery in Boston.

1962

JANUARY 15–FEBRUARY 24. Work included in *USA-FSA: Farm Security Administration Photographs of the Depression Era* at the Allen R. Hite Art Institute, University of Louisville.

SPRING–EARLY FALL. Series of ulcer attacks.

OCTOBER 18–NOVEMBER 25. Eighty-five photographs included in *The Bitter Years* at The Museum of Modern Art.

DECEMBER. Joins Taylor, who is visiting professor at the University of Alexandria, Egypt.

Portrait Photographers of America gives Lange national award "for her international contribution to humanity through photography."

1963

JANUARY 26–MARCH 3. *Death of a Valley* at Art Institute of Chicago.

Recurrent illness in Middle and Near East. Hospitalized in Iran. Taken to Stuttgart and Switzerland. Hospitalized at Interlaken for three weeks with malaria.

MAY 29. Placed on Honor Roll of American Society of Magazine Photographers.

SEPTEMBER 23. Returns to United States.

1964

With John Szarkowski works toward retrospective exhibition of her work at The Museum of Modern Art, to open January 25, 1966.

SPRING. Goes to Washington and New York; proposes independent documentary unit to record American urban life. "Project One," described in long memo, would document the life of the American people in the 1960s with particular emphasis on urban and suburban life.

AUGUST. Illness diagnosed as cancer of the esophagus; receives cobalt therapy.

Completes the portfolio *The American Country Woman.*

Works with KQED (San Francisco) on two thirty-minute films for National Educational Television and Radio Center.

1965

Meets Irwin Welcher, printer of *Family of Man* exhibition, who prints her Museum of Modern Art exhibition.

OCTOBER 11. Dies of cancer, in San Francisco.

Selected Bibliography

Allan R. Hite Art Institute. *USA-FSA, Farm Security Administration Photographs of the Depression Era.* Louisville, Kentucky: University of Louisville, 1962.

"*An American Exodus: A Record of Human Erosion,* by Dorothea Lange and Paul Schuster Taylor" (book review). *U.S. Camera* 1:9 (May 1940):62.

Anderson, James C.; Kytle, Calvin; and Doherty, Robert J. *Roy Stryker: The Humane Propagandist.* Louisville, Kentucky: University of Louisville Photographic Archives, 1977.

Anderson, Sherwood. *Home Town: Photographs by Farm Security Photographers.* New York: Alliance, 1940.

Baldwin, C. "*Documentary Expression and Thirties America,* by William Stott" (book review). *Artforum* 13 (May 1974):67-68.

Baldwin, Sidney. *Poverty and Politics: The Rise and Decline of the Farm Security Administration.* Chapel Hill: University of North Carolina Press, 1968.

Barnitz, Jacqueline. "Dorothea Lange" [review of the exhibition at The Museum of Modern Art]. *Arts* 40:6 (April 1966):53.

Benson, John. "The Dorothea Lange Retrospective, The Museum of Modern Art, New York." *Aperture* 12:4 (1965):40-57.

Busch, Arthur J. "Fellowships for Photographers." *Popular Photography* 11:4 (October 1942):22.

Coke, Van Deren. "Dorothea Lange, Compassionate Recorder." *Modern Photography* 37 (May 1973):90-95.

Coleman, A. D. "A Dark Day in History." *New York Times,* 24 September 1972, Section D, p. 19.

Conrat, Maisie, and Conrat, Richard. *Executive Order 9066: The Internment of 110,000 Japanese Americans.* Cambridge, Mass.: Massachusetts Institute of Technology, 1972.

———. *The American Farm: A Photographic History.* Boston: Houghton Mifflin Company and California Historical Society, 1977.

________________. "Dorothea Lange and Her Printer." *Popular Photography* 59:1 (July 1966):28.

________________. "Lange and Conrat, a Relationship of Conflict but Great Productivity." *Popular Photography* 70:6 (June 1972):32.

Dixon, Daniel. "Dorothea Lange." *Modern Photography* 16:12 (December 1952):68.

Doherty, Robert J., Jr. "U.S.A.-F.S.A.: Farm Security Administration Photographs of the Depression Era." *Camera* 41:10 (October 1962):7, 9-51, cover ill.

"Dorothea Lange." Obituary in *Berkeley Daily Gazette*, 13 October 1965.

Dorothea Lange. Introduction by George Elliott. New York: The Museum of Modern Art, 1966.

"Dorothea Lange." In *Great Photographers*, pp. 184-87. Life Library of Photography. New York: Time-Life, 1971.

Frakenstein, Alfred. "A Lone Lady with a Camera." *San Francisco Chronicle*, 16 July 1978, p. 46.

French, Warren. *Film Guide to "The Grapes of Wrath."* Bloomington: Indiana University Press, 1973.

"F.S.A. Historische Bilddokumente aus den U.S.A." *Fotografie* 19:7 (July 1965): 246-51.

Garver, Thomas H. *Just Before the War: Urban America from 1935 to 1941.* Boston: Newport Harbor Art Museum, 1968.

Gernsheim, Helmut. *Creative Photography: Aesthetic Trends, 1839-1960.* London: Faber & Faber, 1962.

Getlein, Frank. "Paintings and Photographs." *New Republic,* 19 March 1966, pp. 33-35.

Goldsmith, Arthur. "A Harvest of Truth: The Dorothea Lange Retrospective Exhibition." *Infinity* 15:3 (March 1966):23-30.

Gruber, L. Fritz. "Dorothea Lange." In *Grosse Photographen unseres jahrhunderts,* pp. 68-73. Darmstadt: Deutsche Buch-Gemeinschaft, 1964.

Gutman, Judith M. *Lewis Hine and the American Social Conscience.* New York: Walker, 1967.

Herz, Nat. "Dorothea Lange in Perspective: A Reappraisal of the Farm Security Administration and an Interview." *Infinity* 12:4 (April 1963):5-11.

Heyman, Therese Thau. "Looking at Lange Today." *Exposure: The Journal of the Society for Photographic Education* 16:2 (Summer 1978):26-33.

________________. *Celebrating a Collection: The Work of Dorothea Lange.* Oakland, California: The Oakland Museum, 1978.

Howe, Hartley E. "You Have Seen Their Pictures." *Survey Graphic* 29:4 (April 1940):236-41.

________________. *Portrait of a Decade.* Baton Rouge: Louisiana State University Press, 1972.

Issler, Anne Roller. "Good Neighbors Lend a Hand: Our Mexican Workers." *Survey Graphic* 32:10 (December 1943):389-94.

Kehl, D. G. "Steinbeck's 'String of Pictures' in *The Grapes of Wrath." Image* 17:1 (March 1974):1-10.

Kozloff, Max. "Territory of Photographs." *Artforum* 13 (November 1974):64-67.

[Lange, Dorothea]. "A Selection of Some of the Best Photographs of Migrant Workers, 1935-1936." Washington, D.C.: Library of Congress: Selective Checklist of Prints and Photographs. Lot no. 4699, p. 65.

Lange, Dorothea. "Documentary Photography," A Pageant of Photography. In *San Francisco: Palace of Fine Arts.* San Francisco: Crocker-Union, 1949.

________________. "Irish Country People." *Life,* 21 March 1955, pp. 135-43.

________________. "The Assignment I'll Never Forget: Migrant Mother." *Popular Photography* 46:2 (February 1960):42.

________________. "The American Farm Woman." *Harvester World* 51:11 (November 1960):2-9.

________________. "Women of the American Farm." *America Illustrated* (U.S.I.A.), Russian ed. 70 (November 1962):56-61.

________________. Tribute to Charles Russell. In *Paper Talk: Illustrated Letters of Charles M. Russell,* edited by Frederic Renner, p. 3, cover ill. Fort Worth: Amon Carter Museum of Western Art, 1962.

________________. "Remembrance of Asia." In *Photography Annual 1964,* pp. 50-59. New York: Ziff-Davis, 1963.

________________. Interview with Richard K. Doud. Detroit: Archives of American Art, 22 May 1964.

________________. *Dorothea Lange Looks at the American Country Woman.* Commentary by Beaumont Newhall. Los Angeles: Amon Carter Museum at Fort Worth and Ward Ritchie Press, 1967.

________________. *The Making of a Documentary Photographer.* Interview (conducted 1960-61) by Suzanne Riess. Berkeley: Regional Oral History Office, The Bancroft Library, University of California, 1968.

Lange, Dorothea, and Adams, Ansel. "Fortune's Wheel." *Fortune* 31:2 (February 1945):10.

________________. "Three Mormon Towns." *Life,* 6 September 1954, pp. 91-100.

Lange, Dorothea, and Dixon, Daniel. "Photographing the Familiar." *Aperture* 1:2 (1952):4-15.

Lange, Dorothea, and Jones, Pirkle. "Death of a Valley." *Aperture* 8:3 (1960):127-65.

Lange, Dorothea, and Taylor, Paul Schuster. *An American Exodus: A Record of Human Erosion.* Rev. ed. New Haven and London: Yale University Press in association with The Oakland Museum, 1969.

Lenz, Herm. "Interview with Three Greats." *U.S. Camera* 18:8 (August 1955):84-87.

Levin, Howard M., and Northrup, Katherine, eds. *Dorothea Lange: Farm Security Photographs, 1935–1939.* 2 vols. Glencoe, Illinois: The Text-Fiche Press, 1980.

Life: Documentary Photography. Life Library of Photography. New York: Time-Life, 1972.

Lorentz, Pare. "Dorothea Lange: Camera with a Purpose." In *U.S. Camera 1941: America,* vol. I, pp. 93-116, 229. New York: Duell, Sloan & Pearce, 1941.

MacLeish, Archibald. *Land of the Free.* New York: Harcourt, Brace, 1938.

Meltzer, Milton. *Dorothea Lange: A Photographer's Life.* New York: Farrar, Straus & Giroux, 1978.

Miller, Wayne. Obituary of Dorothea Lange. *Camera* 4 (April 1966).

________________. "Dorothea Lange." Unpublished eulogy distributed by Magnum Photos, 1965.

"Miss Lange's Counsel: Photographer Advises Use of Picture Themes." *New York Times,* 7 December 1952, Section II, p. 23.

Mitchell, Margaretta, and Lange, Dorothea. *To a Cabin.* New York: Grossman, 1973.

Morrison, Chester. "Dorothea Lange: Friend of Vision." *Look,* 22 March 1966, pp. 34-38.

Newhall, Beaumont. *The History of Photography: From 1839 to the Present Day.* New York: The Museum of Modern Art, 1949.

Newhall, Beaumont, and Newhall, Nancy. "Dorothea Lange." In *Masters of Photography,* pp.140-49. New York: Braziller, 1958.

Nixon, Herman Clarence. *Forty Acres and Steel Mules.* Chapel Hill: University of North Carolina, 1938.

Ohrn, Karin B. "Prodigal Photography: Professionals Returning to the Home Mode." Paper read at Conference on Culture and Communication, March 1975, at Temple University, Philadelphia, Pennsylvania.

——————. *Dorothea Lange and the Documentary Tradition.* Baton Rouge: Louisiana State University Press, 1980.

O'Neal, Hank. *A Vision Shared: A Classic Portrait of America and Its People 1935-43.* New York: St. Martin's Press, 1976.

Page, Homer. "A Remembrance of Dorrie." *Infinity* 14:11 (November 1965):26-27.

——————. "John Simon Guggenheim Memorial Foundation Fellows in Photography, 1937-1965." *Camera* 45 (April 1966):6.

Penny, Lucretia. "Pea-Picker's Child." *Survey Graphic* 24:7 (July 1935):352-53.

Photography 64: An Invitational Exhibition Co-Sponsored by the New York State Exposition and the George Eastman House. Rochester: Eastman House, 1964.

Photojournalism. Life Library of Photography. New York: Time-Life, 1971.

Pratt, Davis, ed. *The Photographic Eye of Ben Shahn.* Cambridge, Massachusetts: Harvard University Press, 1975.

Report of the President's Committee: Farm Tenancy. Washington, D.C.: Superintendent of Public Documents, edition J129512, February 1937.

Riess, Suzanne, and Chall, Malca. *Paul Schuster Taylor: California Social Scientist.* Interviews conducted 1970-72. Berkeley: Regional Oral History Office, The Bancroft Library, University of California, 1975.

Sekula, Allan. "On the Invention of Photographic Meaning." *Artforum* 13 (January 1975):36-45.

Severin, Werner Joseph. "Photographic Documentation by the Farm Security Administration, 1935-1942." M.A. thesis, Columbia: School of Journalism, University of Missouri, 1959.

——————. "Cameras with a Purpose: The Photojournalists of FSA." *Journalism Quarterly* 41:2 (Spring 1964):191-200.

Smith, W. Eugene. "One Whom I Admire, Dorothea Lange (1895-1965)." *Popular Photography* 58:2 (February 1966):86-88.

Stackpole, Peter. "The Camera as a Sociological Weapon." *U.S. Camera* (May 1966):16, 18.

Steichen, Edward. "The F.S.A. Photographers." In *U.S. Camera 1939,* pp. 43-65. New York: William Morrow, 1938.

——————. "Photography." In *Masters of Modern Art,* edited by Alfred H. Barr, Jr. pp. 183-198. New York: The Museum of Modern Art, 1954.

——————. *The Family of Man.* New York: The Museum of Modern Art and Simon & Schuster, 1955.

——————, ed. *The Bitter Years 1935-1941: Rural America as Seen by the Photographers of the Farm Security Administration.* New York: The Museum of Modern Art, 1962.

Stoddard, Hope. *Famous American Women.* New York: Crowell, 1970.

Stott, William. *Documentary Expression and Thirties America.* New York: Oxford University Press, 1973.

Stryker, Roy Emerson, and Wood, Nancy. *In This Proud Land: America 1935-1943 as Seen in the FSA Photographs.* Greenwich, Connecticut: New York Graphic Society, 1973.

Taylor, Paul Schuster. "Again the Covered Wagon." *Survey Graphic* 24:7 (July 1935):348.

——————. "From the Ground Up." *Survey Graphic* 25:9 (September 1936):524.

——————. "Our Stakes in the Japanese Exodus." *Survey Graphic* 31:9 (September 1942):372.

——————. "Migrant Mother: 1936." *American West* (May 1970):41-47.

Taylor, Paul Schuster, and Gold, Norman Leon. "San Francisco and the General Strike." *Survey Graphic* 23:9 (September 1934):404-411.

Terkel, Studs. *Hard Times: An Oral History of the Great Depression.* New York: Pantheon Books, 1970.

Tucker, Anne, ed. *The Woman's Eye.* New York: Knopf, 1973.

Van Dyke, Willard. "The Photographs of Dorothea Lange: A Critical Analysis." *Camera Craft,* 41:10 (October 1934):461-67.

Films

Green, Philip, and Katz, Robert. *Dorothea Lange, Part One: Under the Trees,* and *Dorothea Lange, Part Two: The Closer for Me.* KQED Film Unit Production: June, 1965 (16mm b/w, sound, 30 minutes each part).

Schulz-Keil, Wieland. *Bread and Roses. A New Deal for the Arts 1935-1943. Part IV: Photography* (16mm color, sound, 45 minutes).

Xerox Films. *A Woman's Place.* (16mm color, sound, 52 minutes).

Acknowledgments

The author and editors of *Dorothea Lange: Photographs of a Lifetime* are grateful to The Oakland Museum for access to its archive of photographs, unpublished notes, letters, and other papers by and about Dorothea Lange, and for assistance in the completion of this project. We acknowledge especially the guidance of Therese Heyman, curator, who contributed invaluable advice and expertise, and Sara Beckner, archival assistant, for her editorial work on the chronology and for researching the photographs. Eddy Dyba printed the photographs from Dorothea Lange's original negatives. John Kelley, supervisor, Information Unit, Photo Duplication Service, The Library of Congress, was generous in providing prints from the Farm Security Administration files. Willard Van Dyke graciously gave permission to reproduce his article on Dorothea Lange which originally appeared in *Camera Craft*. Shirley C. Burden, a close friend of Dorothea Lange's, provided invaluable guidance at every stage of the project. Primary sources for information regarding Dorothea Lange's life and work include: the biography by Milton Meltzer (*Dorothea Lange: A Photographer's Life,* New York: Farrar, Straus & Giroux, 1978), Karin Becker Ohrn's *Dorothea Lange and the Documentary Tradition* (Baton Rouge: Louisiana State University Press, 1980), and Zoe Brown's studies of Dorothea Lange's field notes.